THE EDUCATION OF
CORPORAL JOHN MUSGRAVE

THE EDUCATION OF
Corporal
John Musgrave

Vietnam and Its Aftermath

JOHN MUSGRAVE

 ALFRED A. KNOPF | NEW YORK | 2021

THIS IS A BORZOI BOOK
PUBLISHED BY ALFRED A. KNOPF

Copyright © 2021 by John Musgrave
Foreword copyright © 2021 by Lynn Novick and Ken Burns

All rights reserved. Published in the United States by Alfred A. Knopf,
a division of Penguin Random House LLC, New York, and distributed in Canada
by Penguin Random House Canada Limited, Toronto.

www.aaknopf.com

Knopf, Borzoi Books, and the colophon
are registered trademarks of Penguin Random House LLC.

All photographs are courtesy of the author unless otherwise indicated.

Library of Congress Cataloging-in-Publication Data
Names: Musgrave, John, [date] author.
Title: The education of Corporal John Musgrave : Vietnam and its aftermath /
John Musgrave.
Description: First edition. | New York : Alfred A. Knopf, 2021.
Identifiers: LCCN 2020021754 (print) | LCCN 2020021755 (ebook) |
ISBN 9780451493569 (hardcover) | ISBN 9780451493576 (ebook)
Subjects: LCSH: Musgrave, John, 1948– | Vietnam War, 1961–1975—Personal narratives,
American. | United States. Marine Corps—Biography. | United States. Marine Corps.
Marine Regiment, 9th. | Vietnam War, 1961–1975—Veterans—Biography. |
Vietnam War, 1961–1975—Protest movements—United States. |
Veterans—United States—Social conditions—20th century.
Classification: LCC DS559.5 .M876 2021 (print) | LCC DS559.5 (ebook) |
DC 959.7/0434092 [B]—dc23
LC record available at https://lccn.loc.gov/2020021754
LC ebook record available at https://lccn.loc.gov/2020021755ata}

Jacket photograph courtesy of the author
Jacket design by Tyler Comrie

Manufactured in Canada
First Edition

To my parents, Robert and Wilda Musgrave
If we're truly blessed we get two families:
The one God grants us at birth,
and the other we build with the people
God places in our lives.
It's all about family.
Semper Fi

Certainly there is no hunting like the hunting of man and those who have hunted armed men long enough and liked it, never really care for anything else thereafter. You will meet them doing various things with resolve, but their interest rarely holds because after the other thing ordinary life is as flat as the taste of wine when the taste buds have been burned off your tongue.

—ERNEST HEMINGWAY, "On the Blue Water"

Contents

Foreword

For more than a decade, we tried to make sense of one of the most consequential, divisive, and unsettled events in American history. We hoped, in the process of creating our documentary film series *The Vietnam War,* we would find answers to many essential questions: What really happened? Why did things go wrong? Who is to blame? Why, four decades after it ended, are we unable to put Vietnam behind us? And why, long after our government reconciled with the government of our former enemy, have we not yet fully reconciled among ourselves? While making our film, we got to know more than a hundred men and women who bravely shared their stories with us, Americans and Vietnamese, combatants and civilians. Seeing the war through their eyes, we came to understand that our initial questions led only to deeper, sometimes unanswerable questions: Were the sacrifices in blood and bone too high? What meaning can be found in the trauma and suffering of the war? Who was right? Who was wrong? And, ultimately, what does it mean to be a patriot, and a hero?

Of all the human beings who bore witness for our cameras and helped us see and hear and appreciate the nuances and complexities of the war, none touched us more deeply than John Musgrave. From Lynn's first phone call with John in 2010, we realized we were in the presence of one of the most

honest, brave, thoughtful, decent, selfless, and compassion-
ate human beings we have ever had the good fortune to know.
Spending time with John, being present as he told his devas-
tating and inspiring story, was humbling, overwhelming, life
altering. There are no words, truly, to express our gratitude for
the priceless gift he gave to our project, and to posterity. As he
recounted his epic journey from innocent young man to hardened Marine, grievously wounded warrior, impassioned antiwar protester, and finally aging veteran, we were spellbound.
Throughout, John was, and is, unfailingly, scrupulously, honest.
John cannot *not* tell the truth, whether it puts him in the best
light or not. And sometimes, as he will be the first to tell you, it
does not. Having interviewed him and spent a lot of time with
him, we thought we knew John's story, but the revelation of this
beautiful and wrenching memoir is that, in collaboration with
the brilliant writer Bryan Doerries, John has found the courage to dig even deeper. He peels back the layers of his life, and
his soul, to revisit his most searing experiences in the war, his
alienation as a Vietnam veteran on a college campus, his search
for meaning and purpose in an increasingly polarized and atom-
ized America, and his determination to impart his wisdom to
younger generations of Soldiers so that they do not have to
endure the same suffering he went through. In sharing his intimate personal odyssey so completely in this book, John Musgrave has given us yet another great gift: he has shown us what
it really means to be a patriot and a hero.

Ken Burns and Lynn Novick

THE EDUCATION OF
CORPORAL JOHN MUSGRAVE

The Music of the Night

EVERY MARINE HAS THREE BIRTHDAYS: the day his mother issued him onto this earth, the day the Marine Corps was formed—November 10, 1775—and the day he graduated from boot camp and was addressed for the first time as a Marine. On that day, he is reborn and everything in his life irrevocably changes.

It is said that the Marine Corps builds men, at least that was the slogan when I enlisted at age seventeen, but not one of us who entered boot camp together in 1966 was foolish enough to think he would be a man when it was over. We would be Marines, and that was enough for us. Still, I don't think we realized how dramatic the transformation would be.

The Corps specializes in tearing down recruits and remolding them as Marines. At boot camp, the Drill Instructors work tirelessly to undo nearly two decades of civilian bullshit in new recruits. And that's exactly what they did to me. When they were done, I was completely different, inside and out.

Me in my Boy Scout uniform, next to my brother, Butch,
in front of my home in Fairmount, Missouri, in 1959.

I entered boot camp skinny and tall, and when I left, I was thirty pounds heavier and one inch taller. My waist remained the same, because I had gained nothing but muscle. But even more pronounced than these physical changes was my new attitude, a whole new sense of self-worth, self-confidence, and mission.

During boot camp, I had been challenged—physically and mentally—like never before, and I had risen to the challenge. I learned to deliver violence upon fellow human beings—not just how to kill, but how to cultivate the requisite attitude and willingness to pull the trigger. And, over the course of those thirteen weeks, my friends and I had also acquired a deep and abiding sense of loyalty, to each other and to the Corps. As a child, I had a vague notion of loyalty from Boy Scouts and church, but the Marine Corps hammered it into us—clear and strong—like the steel of a bayonet. If we learned one thing in boot camp, it was the value of loyalty, that Marines never abandon their buddies, no matter what. I, and thousands of other Marines, wouldn't be here today if it weren't for that lesson or for the system that created the young men who were willing to die to help a buddy.

When we graduated, I remember feeling that I had 190 years of tradition behind me, supporting me, and pushing me forward. I would never quit. I would never surrender. For if I did, I would be failing, not just the Corps, but my fellow Marines, who were more important to me than anyone I had ever known. And that's why I do everything I do today, to help other veterans and those who are suffering. That is why I am writing this book, with the hope that it might someday help someone who is lost or lonely find his way home. It has taken me fifty years to finally feel as if I've come back from the war, and I know I'm not alone in my sense of isolation.

Countless times since I returned from Vietnam, people have approached me, in all sincerity, and asked, "Why don't you just try to forget what happened? Why can't you just leave it behind?" Each time this happens, I am stunned by the audacity of the question. *If you have to ask me why, then I'm not sure I can explain it to you.* But they don't know what they're asking. In suggesting that I forget, they are telling me to leave behind the men with whom I experienced the war. To forget them would be the greatest act of betrayal. It is my duty to do everything I can to remember. As they say in the bush, as long as there's one of us left to tell the story, nobody dies. This book is a willful act of remembrance in honor of my friends, some who didn't make it back, others who are still finding their way home. I'm still trying to live up to the lessons they taught me.

September 2016 marked the fiftieth anniversary of my arrival at Marine Corps Recruit Depot, San Diego. Two of my closest

*Jay Van Velzen, right, and me at a surprise going-away party
before we left for boot camp on August 30.*

buddies—Jay Van Velzen and Skip Combs—and I wanted to go
back, not just for graduation, but during the same time of year
in which we had trained. So we maxed out our credit cards and
set out to retrace our steps, traveling there by train, the same
way we had originally traveled as kids. To travel by train is to go
back in time, to see America as it has always been, far from the
highway, untouched.

Back in 1966, there were five of us from my senior class at Van
Horn High School in Independence, Missouri, who enlisted.
First, Jay and I signed up. Then three of our friends decided
to join. There were six others from two rival high schools who
made the journey by rail to California with us and ended up
being in our platoon. At the time, we had no idea what a bless-
ing it was to travel by train, which gave us nearly three days
to reflect upon the fact that we were now far from home and
embarking on a life-changing experience. They assigned two

men per compartment, so Jay—my closest friend in the whole world—and I had a compartment to ourselves.

On the way, we met a young Marine who was returning to Camp Pendleton after being home on leave. Naturally, we peppered him with a million questions and grew even more nervous with each of his answers. This was the first adult thing that any of us had done, and it was not lost on us that there was a war going on and casualties were ramping up. To be honest, I was excited by the danger. The last thing I wanted was to be bored, and the war seemed like the ultimate adventure. Fifty years later, that air of excitement and anticipation was still present, but this time it resulted from three older men going back to revisit one of the most formative experiences of their lives.

One of the best aspects of traveling by train is that no one is in a hurry to get to his destination. Everyone knows that the journey is part of the experience and that meeting people and sharing stories only enrich the trip. I had forgotten this and was thrilled to rediscover it on the way to San Diego. Skip had boarded the train in Kansas City the night before, and Jay and I got picked up in Lawrence, Kansas, around midnight. By the next morning, word had already spread throughout the train cars that three Vietnam veterans were making the journey back to where their journey had started.

On the trip out to San Diego, because we had purchased our tickets at different times, Skip and I had a sleeper compartment, but Jay had been relegated to a seat at the rear of the train. Skip and I would walk back to see him, and people began saying things like "Are you the buddy of that Marine in the back of the train?" We had been wearing our Marine Corps shirts and talking at top volume, in order for Skip, who is nearly deaf, to hear what we were saying. Naturally, people overheard our banter and became interested. When they caught wind of what we were doing, people would ask, "Do you really want to do that?" "Hell yes!" we replied.

When the conductor, who turned out to have been an Army veteran himself, heard that Jay was having to sleep in a regular seat, separated from his buddies, he came and found us and said, "Your brother shouldn't have to be sitting way back there like that. It ain't right. I got a family getting off at ten thirty tonight, and when they do, their family room will open up. You guys go on and move your gear down there at ten thirty." Then he went back to Jay and said, "I'm not going to have you sleeping in a chair that far away from your buddies. You're going up front with them."

In the dining car, because there were four seats to a table, we'd have a stray passenger with us for every meal. At one meal, an older lady, probably about our age, sat down in the empty seat and inquired, "Are you the men who are going back?" "Yes, ma'am," we replied. "My first boyfriend," she said, "my first true love, was a Marine." She went on to recount how they had been high school sweethearts. Though the relationship hadn't survived his tour in Vietnam, her whole demeanor changed when she talked about him. She was a teenage girl again. "He was a wonderful boy," she told us, "and I was so proud of him."

Later in the trip, as I was walking down the aisle of one of the cars, a guy reached out and stopped me and asked, "Are you one of those Marines that's going back to San Diego for your fiftieth reunion?" When I said yes, he pressed further: "Is it for your platoon or your company or something?" And I said, "No. It's just for the three of us. We grew up together. Joined the Corps together. Went to boot camp together." People couldn't believe what we were doing. The journey amazed them, and it was amazing to see them so amazed.

When we finally arrived at the recruit depot in San Diego, it was striking how little had changed. We were met by the same sounds and smells, the same Spanish colonial and Quonset huts (a few of them had been set aside from the olden days), the same "grinder," our name for the parade ground where they ground us down before building us back up again. Though some of the barracks had been replaced with parking lots, almost everywhere we looked, the depot was suffused with an overwhelming sense of permanence. Walking onto the base was a trip through time, only this round we were returning as old men, with new perspectives on and memories of young friends we had made there who were dead within a year of graduating.

It was thrilling to step off the train and back into our youth, but part of the thrill was that we weren't met by Drill Instructors in their campaign covers—the classic Smokey Bear–style hat—charging in our direction to scare the hell out of us right there in the train station. Instead, we jumped into a cab and zipped straight over to the main gate. When I showed my retired military ID card to the Marine guard, he said, "You're good to go, sir. Welcome aboard," and waved us through. I can't describe how that felt. We all looked at each other and said, "Oorah," the battle cry of the Marines. We were giddy with anticipation, and I was nearly overcome with the enormity of my survival and all that had happened to me within twelve months of graduating.

After all those years, and the countless lives lost, I had been granted the privilege of standing there as a survivor. It was overwhelming. And as I took in the moment, the only thought in my mind was, *I hope I haven't let my buddies down. I hope they're not disappointed with me.* When you survive, you remain loyal to your friends. You don't forget them. Standing there at MCRD San Diego, I realized how fortunate I was to be able to do what every one of them wished he could do but never had the opportunity. I understood that I was there to represent every member of my recruit platoon who had been killed in Vietnam, because everyone who saw us on base would be forming opinions about Marines from our era. It filled me with a sense of purpose and responsibility.

The kids all looked exactly as we did back in the day. They were squared away in the same uniforms and bursting with pride. We had arrived for a graduation, and when many of the newly minted Marines saw us, they approached us with eagerness and curiosity. Talking to them was uncannily like talking to younger versions of ourselves.

The eagerness of the Marines to hear our stories reminded us of how eager we had been to talk to noncommissioned officers, or NCOs, when we were their age, especially NCOs who had served in World War II and Korea. Now we were the NCOs who were representing a war that these guys had been learning about in boot camp, which they probably hadn't even touched in high school history classes, because high school history seldom progresses past World War II. But they study Vietnam in boot camp because we wrote a lot of Marine Corps history in those years, and there are no more Vietnam veterans in the Corps, because we're too old to serve now.

The attention and respect those young Marines paid us was humbling and exhilarating. They had just graduated from boot camp, and the reality of now being Marines was just setting in, as was the fact that there was a war still going on in which they might soon be fighting. No doubt they had heard and read about how vicious the fighting had been in our war. To them, we were a part of ancient history, probably similar to running into a Civil War vet. All of their Marine training was fresh on their minds, and they were primed to learn from us. Their hunger to absorb as much of our shared history as they could was palpable. And speaking with these young Marines brought up things for us—thoughts and memories—that we hadn't talked about in fifty years. I've had a lot of experience talking with veterans of all ages, but I was still floored by the exchange. Skip and Jay, who've had less experience interacting with the younger generation, were practically speechless. (Skip is a politician, and I've never seen him speechless.)

In addition to encountering these young Marines, we were meeting Drill Instructors. Still to this day, whenever a Drill Instructor walks up, no matter how friendly or respectful he appears, my asshole slams shut and I think, *Holy crap. Here it comes.* But we were treated by them with deference and respect, and it was a great feeling to know that we had earned it.

The recruit depot completely transforms after dark. The gates close. Civilians go home. And the recruits return from the grinder to their barracks, where, for the rest of the night, they are at the mercy of their Drill Instructors. Because we were able to stay in the hostess house, where they put up guests on base, we were also able to explore the base at this magical time, when one can hear what we affectionately call the "music of the night," the sounds of Drill Instructors verbally thrashing the recruits and the recruits having to yell back their answers. Around eight o'clock that first night, we decided to amble across the grinder and stand near the recruit barracks, to take in the music of the night.

We were in luck, because we chanced upon a barracks that was loaded with six platoons, all filled with recruits who were in their first training week. This means that they had been at the depot for two weeks, but part of the hell of boot camp is that your first week, which is consumed with administrative activities, doesn't count. It's called zero week, and they never hesitate to let you know that you haven't had your first training day until you've completed the week.

Each platoon is composed of roughly seventy-five recruits. So it's extremely powerful to hear all of those voices, like a Greek chorus, shouting together in unison, especially if yours was one of those voices fifty years ago. There is also a certain musicality to it. Jay, Skip, and I stood out there, listening to those all-too-familiar night sounds, letting them wash over us. Of course, the recruits never got it right the first time, and they never shouted loudly enough. It was the repetition, over and over, of their drills that pumped us up and sent adrenaline coursing through my veins, as if I had just jumped out of an airplane at twelve thousand feet.

All three of us were grooving on each other, like teenagers listening to their favorite band. Poor Skip, who's nearly deaf, could hear through his cochlear implants only a fraction of what we were hearing. So Jay and I kept trying to tell Skip what the recruits were saying. Then, all of a sudden, one of the Drill Instructors peeled off from a platoon and began walking toward us. Drill instructors have a special walk. It's kind of like watching the grim reaper approach. This one had his campaign cover on, and it was cocked low over his eyes, as he marched straight in our direction, giving the impression that the ground shook beneath his every step, though we were the ones who were shaking at the sight of this guy thirty years our junior.

As the Drill Instructor approached us, I looked over at Jay and said, "Stand by." And Jay replied, "Oh, boy," because we thought he was going to come over and ask us what the hell we were doing and then tell us to get our asses out of there. We were prepared to talk about it with him, but it was still intimidating as the Drill Instructor stood at an imposing six five, towering over us, ramrod straight, the creases in his utilities absolutely knife sharp. As soon as he saw us up close, he said he could tell that we were Marines, and not family members who had come for graduation. Drill instructors are aware of the symbolism of their campaign covers, which represent to recruits the ultimate authority, a near godlike status. And even to old Marines it still holds that status and brings back memories. So, as soon as he understood who we were, in a show of respect he took his campaign cover off, in order to relate to us Marine to Marine, and started chatting us up.

We soon learned that his name was Scott Jackson. He was a gunnery sergeant, in his late twenties, who turned out to be a wonderful guy. Drill instructors are the cream of the crop. They have the most important job, the creation of new Marines. And Drill Instructor school is the hardest training in the Corps, because they have to be able to do everything better than the best recruit could ever do. They are the picture of professionalism, the perfect image of a Marine.

After we got to know the gunny and established a friendship with him, he introduced us to other Drill Instructors he wanted us to know so we could see that the Marine Corps was in "perfect hands," a phrase that delighted us when he said it. And in that inimitable Drill Instructor cadence he said, "Well, gentlemen, the verbiage may have changed, but the product, I assure you, is just the same." From what we observed, there was no doubting this, but when we parted ways with him, I couldn't help but hope that in three or four years down the road every one of those kids whose hands I shook, or who acknowledged me with respect, would still be alive.

The day before boot camp graduation is called Family Day, when family members from across the country arrive to watch their kids graduate. The store where they sell Marine Corps–

related materials at the depot is filled with racks of T-shirts saying, "My son's a Marine" or "I'm the grandmother of a Marine"
or "I'm the thirty-second cousin of a Marine." Each of the
platoons had a platoon of parents and loved ones who would
all sit together in T-shirts with their recruit's platoon number
and name on them. One of the shirts that tickled us said, "My
little knucklehead is now a big jarhead." These parents were
motivated and proud, and it seemed as if every little kid we met
was wearing a shirt that said, "I want to be a Marine like my big
brother."

The recruit depot has a museum, devoted to the history of
the depot and the Marines who have served there. For graduation day, Jay and I had T-shirts made for the three of us, featuring the First Battalion, Ninth Marines emblem, along with
the grim reaper and the phrase "The Walking Dead." Mine
had "Con Thien" written in orange across the top, and "Vietnam 1967" below it. Jay's had the First Tank, First Marine Division emblem and "Da Nang 1968." That morning, we visited
the depot museum in our specially made T-shirts and walked
around, taking in the exhibits. Each room in the museum represents a different war, and when we got to the Vietnam room, I
was pleased to see that the section on the Marine Corps in 1967
featured a large display on Con Thien, a terrifyingly exposed
outpost two miles below the DMZ in the north of South Vietnam, and also about my unit.

Jay, Skip, and I stood nearly still, deeply moved, in front of a
large photograph that was taken while I served in Con Thien
during the siege, in which hundreds of Marines lost their
lives and thousands more were wounded, depicting a group
of Marines hunkering down in a trench under heavy artillery
fire. The photo, which had been made famous in *Life* magazine,

could have been of my buddies and me. During our time in Con Thien, we were outgunned, outmanned, and surrounded on all sides by three divisions of the North Vietnamese Army. It was like having a big red target painted on us, twenty-four hours a day. The near-constant threat of imminent death never abated, and I lost many of my closest friends on that desolate hill.

A few minutes later, as I began talking to Jay and Skip about what Con Thien had meant to me, I turned around and realized that I was surrounded by a group of young Marines and their families. They were all leaning forward, listening to what we were saying, and some of these young Marines who had just walked up were whispering to their mothers and fathers, "This guy, this Marine, was at Con Thien."

They listened with rapt attention as I continued to tell my story and reflected upon my time in Con Thien. This moment was very powerful for me. Time collapsed, and I found myself occupying three places at once. I was standing on the battlefield in Con Thien; in the recruit depot museum talking to the Marines; and outside myself, as a young Marine, listening to a veteran share his war stories. Looking at those young faces in the small crowd that had gathered around us was like looking into a mirror. It was as if, fifty years ago, there had been a veteran talking to me about the Chosin Reservoir in Korea and I was listening with the same eagerness and pride. I knew what these kids were feeling, because I had felt it once myself. And I thought, *Holy shit. I've lived to see the day when a young Marine would look upon me with awe. We were finally old enough to be called Old Corps.*

They weren't just looking at me. They were looking at every Marine Vietnam veteran who looked just like them when he graduated from boot camp but didn't get to come home. The respect they were conveying that morning went a long way to healing a pretty big wound that I've been carrying since my return from the war. The museum had served its purpose, connecting the past with the present in a very real and tangible way. Something about this brief moment of recognition and connection expanded me.

As we left the museum, Skip, Jay, and I were all a little dazed. None of us had expected to be affirmed and even welcomed home, in a way, by those young Marines and their families. We were as awestruck by them as they were by us. And it is with this same sense of reverence and awe, for all those who wear or have worn the uniform, that I write this book, with the ambition that it will inspire the same feeling in others and help veterans of every generation find words for their stories and an audience of concerned, engaged citizens who are ready to listen.

BOOK ONE
——

THE MAKING OF A MARINE

CHAPTER 1

Born to Serve

Second grade, 1956.

S ERVICE WAS IN MY DNA from the very beginning. I was born because of my parents' service, and I was born to serve. World War II brought my mother and father together, compelling them both to join the effort right after the United States declared war against Japan. My father served as a Pilot and my mother as a secretary at a nearby aviation plant, where they first met. So, in a very real way, my older brother, Butch, and I both owe our lives to the bombing of Pearl Harbor.

My first conscious memory of our nation being at war was forged when I was just three or four years old, around 1951.

Butch and I preparing to "watch the radio," 1950.

Butch and I were too young to read the newspaper, so our news came from the newsreels that were shown at the community movie theater in Fairmount, Missouri, just down the road from where we lived. Almost every weekend, our parents would take us to Saturday matinees, terrible westerns and sometimes cartoons. We'd stay there all day drinking sodas and eating popcorn and candy bars, as many as we could afford. Sometimes all our parents could buy us were the tickets, which went for ten cents a pop. It was in that theater that I first saw images of the Korean War. I still have indelibly vivid memories of black-and-white footage of men in combat, with a vague understanding that my father and my uncles had also served in places like that.

The kids growing up in my community were all aware of the military, and we were the first generation to be fully aware of the draft. Most of the boys and girls in my neighborhood were the grandchildren of World War I veterans, and I don't recall a

My dad with a group of Pilots and a biplane. Dad is on the far right.

friend whose father wasn't a veteran of World War II or Korea. Some even served in both. Though my grandfathers hadn't served in World War I—Grandpa Musgrave was legally blind and couldn't serve; Grandpa Bartlett was drafted right before the war ended and never got called up—I was still admired by my peers, because my father had served as a Pilot and an officer. So naturally I played that up, and I had big dreams of growing up to become a waist gunner on my dad's B-17 bomber, known as the Flying Fortress. That was my first military fantasy, around age eight, to be a crewman on my father's plane. Eventually, when I finally accepted that B-17s weren't flying anymore and my father wasn't flying either, I was terribly disappointed and started casting about for another way to serve my country.

I had no interest in superheroes as a child, because my friends and I were surrounded by real heroes every day. My father was Superman to me. From an early age, I understood that he had helped save the world. We didn't know much about the Germans, but we knew they did horrible things. We knew they shot prisoners, tortured American servicemen, and killed innocent people, but we had no idea just how many people or of the scale of destruction left in their path.

I don't recall anyone telling me that they hated the Germans. Some veterans even spoke about them with pride, saying that they were good Soldiers and they were glad they fought against them. However, when it came to the Japanese, among my parents' generation there was a deep-seated anger and distrust. My father often said that he would never forgive the Japanese for Pearl Harbor, Bataan, and Corregidor. If pressed, he would say that he "didn't like 'em or trust 'em." When I reflect back on it now, the conduct of the Japanese Soldiers across the Pacific was bestial, and the hatred it engendered made some sense. What was unforgivable was demonizing our own citizens of Japanese descent and holding them responsible for the war and imprisoning them.

We had a friend, Bob Landry, who had been on the USS *Oklahoma* on December 7, 1941, at Pearl Harbor. He had been wounded that fateful Sunday morning, and so the attack was very real for us and for most of the people in our community. When we heard stories about war on the news, the reporters were talking about our Scout masters, about friends' fathers, about my minister, who was a chaplain in World War II, and about our male teachers, of whom there were few because of the wars.

We wanted to be just like these veterans, and as we got older, it seemed as if at every party, while the women gathered in the living room, a group of men would huddle in the kitchen, drinking and swapping war stories. Whenever I could, I would go stand in the doorway and eavesdrop. Oftentimes, the things I heard them say were a lot different from what they might say if they knew I was standing there. Among themselves, they were pretty open. They talked of the places they had been, and of battles I was seeing on TV or in the movies. These were just regular guys from the neighborhood, but they had done extraordinary things in the service of their country. Surrounded by these men and their stories, I began to look at adults in a different way, with respect and with a curiosity to know what they had done in the war.

When I was in high school, I had a teacher named Mr. West who wore thick glasses and walked hunched over and with a slow gait. He talked slowly, almost as if he were mentally impaired, but he was actually a very intelligent man. All of my classmates were merciless when it came to Mr. West, saying cruel things about him, but I never did. He was a good teacher and he knew his subject, American history, well, and for that he commanded my respect. Once day, while I was talking with him about an assignment, he shared with me that he had been wounded in combat. To that point, I had never thought of him as a veteran, because he didn't match up to the picture that I had of veterans. It turned out that he had served as an Army infantry officer in Korea. When his jeep ran over a land mine, he sustained a skull facture, a broken back, and a fragmentation wound. From that point on, anytime I heard anyone dropping shit on old Mr. West, I would stand up for him and say that he had been wounded fighting for us and we had no right to make fun of him. After that, I never made assumptions about who people were or what they had experienced.

The father of a friend had been in the Marine Corps. To my surprise, my friend's mother had also been in the Corps. It's where his parents had met and married. She was one of the very few female veterans I met when I was a kid. I was aware that most women had done something to assist the war effort, and because of my mother's role during World War II, I was never allowed to think that women didn't participate. From an early age, I started judging people, especially men, based upon their military service, or lack thereof. If they hadn't served in any way, I wasn't very interested in what they had to say. I just couldn't understand why they hadn't served. I'm sure they all had good reasons, but to my young mind everybody served, period. If you didn't, well, in a certain way, it was inexcusable.

In my father's community in Frankfort, Kansas, there was a kid who, although he was eligible for the draft, somehow got out of it. His father said he was essential to the family farm, and so the kid stayed home, raised crops, and prospered. Because there had been no interruption to his life, he became very wealthy, as he had been able to capitalize upon the sacrifices of other boys his age. While they were away fighting, he remained home and dated all the girls those guys were dreaming of overseas, because he was one of the few able-bodied guys in town. My dad and his buddies, who were all veterans, never forgave this guy for taking the easy way out. If they ran into him in a restaurant, they would make it obvious that they wanted nothing to do with him. And if he tried to talk to them, they'd blow him off. I remember thinking I didn't ever want to be that guy, the guy who didn't serve when everybody else did. I thought that heroes serve their country and cowards find their way out of service.

I started haunting the Marine Corps recruiting station in Independence, Missouri, when I was thirteen years old. Over time, I came to know the recruiters pretty well. One of them, Gunnery Sergeant Matthews, who had served in World War II and Korea, looked like an English bulldog. I went down to the office for the first time in February of eighth grade, when I was four feet, eleven inches tall, and offered up to the recruiters in my prepubescent voice, "I'm gonna be a Marine." They weren't totally discouraging, but they did tell me to come back when I had "grown a set of balls" and "put on a little more weight."

In February 1966, my senior year of high school, I returned to the recruiting station to pick up some Marine Corps magazines and posters for my room. By this time, I had grown a bit and my voice had finally dropped, but I still had a long way to go before I imagined I would be Marine material. When Gunny Matthews saw me, though, he immediately asked if I was seventeen yet. When I told him I was, he fired back, "Well, then, are you going to join the Corps today?" Unable to form a sentence, I sputtered. All I had wanted my entire life was to be a Marine. Asking me if I wanted to join the Corps was like asking me if I wanted to play in the Beach Boys. When I finally regained my wits, I said something to the effect of "Hell yeah!" and plopped down in a chair right next to Gunny Matthews's desk. He pulled out this huge stack of forms and said, "Let's get her done."

Given my age, we both knew that he would still have to come to my home and persuade my parents to sign, but he wanted to get my commitment down in writing then and there so that all my parents would have to do was agree. Once we'd signed all those papers and they obtained my parents' permission, there would be no turning back. Gunny Matthews had a strategy and a plan, and he caught me flat-footed when I walked into his office that day.

First, he told me, "We've got to decide your obligation," which meant how many years of service I'd be signing up for that day. Gunny Matthews laid out the options: reserves for five and a half years, a three-year program of active duty, a four-year program, and even a six-year obligation, of which four could be active and two could be inactive, reserve, where you didn't have to go to anything but could be called up anytime. After hearing all the options, I said, "Hell, give me twenty. I want to be a career Marine." He laughed and said, "Okay, well, I tell you what. Why don't we just start out with four?" And I said, "Okay, that sounds like a good deal to me," but I was ready to sign the rest of my life away to the U.S. Marines.

I was nervous sitting in front of that pile of paperwork. In fact, I was so shaken and excited that I managed to misspell my own name on the first three forms he gave me. The first time, I thought, *Okay, that was weird. That won't happen again,* but then I repeated the mistake two more times. When he pointed it out, I was embarrassed. Of course, it wasn't lost on me that I was, in that very moment, achieving a lifelong dream. I was also well aware that there was a war going on and I could very well be signing my obituary. Though it was still early in the war, the impact of the conflict was already being felt in Independence, Missouri, because many young men from my school and community had enlisted, had trained, and were fighting overseas. There had been close to two thousand American casualties in Vietnam in 1965, including one of my classmates from Van Horn High School, Bill Peck, a tall kid with reddish-blond hair whom I had known since eighth grade. As sobering as that was, I was still thrilled about the prospect of going to war. It made enlisting a lot more intense, but it also ensured that I wouldn't end up sitting on my ass for four years at Camp Pendleton, running drills and training endlessly to go to war but never getting to fight in one. I knew that if I really wanted to serve my country, I needed to be there when I was needed the most, which was then, in the beginning of 1966, when Marines had been dying in

Vietnam for more than a year. I was determined to go there and prove myself worthy of being called a Marine.

Gunny Matthews handed me my official Marine recruit ID card, which read, "Private John D. Musgrave 2294574 has enlisted in the U.S. Marine Corps." He said, "If you ever get stopped by the police or somebody asks you for identification, you show them this card, and it may get you out of trouble," and it actually did save me from a traffic ticket once. I'd been chasing a girl from church while riding my motorcycle.

I left the recruit station, which was on the Independence town square, and beelined for the bowling alley, just around the corner, to share the news with my best friend, Jay. I walked into the place as plumped up as a Butterball turkey. I was so proud of myself. I glided straight back to the pin machines, where Jay was working. When he saw me, he immediately asked, "What did you do?" because I looked as if I'd obviously done something I was pretty thrilled about. And I said, "I enlisted," to which he replied, "You son of a bitch! You can't go without me." So I said, "Well, then, better hurry the hell up." So Jay stopped what he was doing, went straight down to the recruiting station, and enlisted too. I went home from the bowling alley and told my parents, who were underwhelmed, to say the least. They knew that at seventeen I still needed their signatures to complete the paperwork, so they expected we wouldn't be having the conversation until after I turned eighteen. I caught them off guard that afternoon. They dug in and told me, "Absolutely not," but I pushed back and convinced them they really had no choice in the matter. It was the first time I challenged my father on anything, and once they saw how badly I wanted to be a Marine, they gave in, with the caveat that I had to finish high school before I could go.

When they first heard of my intention to enlist, which I made clear in eighth grade, my parents begged me to go to college instead, and they offered to take out loans. My brother, Butch, had gone to college on scholarship, but due to my mediocre grades I would never qualify for one, and I knew that if I went, all I would do was make my mother, who was very unhappy with her job in the IBM department at the Sheffield Steel Company in Kansas City, work for another few years. It would have been a waste of money, because I was through with school. No more teachers, no more books. I was hell-bent on becoming a Marine. I had to talk like a senator to finally convince my parents that I was right. Mother—God bless her—quit her job right after I left, and it made me feel like a man that I had finally done something that was really helping my family.

Jay was never as ramped up as I was about joining the Corps. His father had served as a Marine and had been wounded on Okinawa; he was proud of his service but never glorified it, often telling Jay that it was a "hard goddamn job" and that he "nearly got killed doing it." So in high school, Jay always said that if you're smart, you joined the Navy or the Air Force, but to me that screamed wimp, and I argued with him about it. Thankfully, Jay determined that if I joined the Marine Corps, he would go with me. He knew that when we graduated from high school, we weren't going to go to college and that in six or ten months, a year at most, he'd be drafted into the Army. He said, "Hell, I don't know if I could even live if you're not here. There won't be anything to do, nobody to hang out with, so I'll just come with you."

From the moment I met him, Jay had always been there for me. His friendship was the best thing that happened in high school. It saved me. During my early adolescence, from about

Me with sax.

fourth grade on, I had been the runt of the litter and struggled to keep up with my peers. During this miserable and deeply humiliating time, I learned all about bullies. Some days it seemed as if nearly every kid at school might take a shot at me, and I was scared to death. I couldn't fight these guys. I was just a little kid, a so-called adolescent male who was never going to have a girlfriend and who lived in near-constant fear of being attacked.

In high school, when all of my classmates were going out for football, track, and basketball, I joined the marching band, and this turned out to be one of the best decisions of my young life. In the saxophone section of the school band that year, there was this blond-headed kid who sat a couple seats down from me named Jay Van Velzen. He was a total cutup, getting into trouble all the time, but it was never anything mean-spirited. He was always just having fun.

I discovered that one of the ways to keep bullies from lashing out at me was to make them laugh. So I'd been working on my comedy routines pretty seriously for a while. It was a matter of survival. This kid Jay was funny as hell, a little irreverent for my taste, but an all-around great guy. I don't know what it was about me that caused him to want to be my friend, because I was pretty square compared with him, but we shared a wry sense of humor and found that we enjoyed each other's company. Before we knew it, we had become good buddies.

My parents adored Jay. Mom loved him because he'd eat anything she'd put in front of him. Because Mom worked almost as much as Dad, her cooking could be a little experimental at times, and our vegetables came out of cans. But the rule at our house was you would take some of everything on the table and you would eat it all. To this day, I'm not sure Jay understands how instrumental our friendship was in my survival in those first two high school years. In him, I found a true friend, someone in whom I could confide, and we really talked, all the time.

The summer after graduating from high school, before leaving for boot camp, my friends and I did everything as though it would be our last time. Better have fun now, we reasoned, in case we don't make it back. And we had an amazing time. Dad took Jay and me to Lake of the Ozarks every chance we got so we could water-ski and chase girls. Jay went with us on family vacations up to my grandparents' farm, in Paradise, Kansas, and all of my relatives considered him part of the family. He was just a Musgrave with a funny last name.

I owned my own motorcycle, from money I earned playing with my rock band, the Fabulous Revells, and Jay rented one that summer and rode with me whenever he could. You could rent a motorcycle for an evening for like five or ten bucks.

Sometimes when Jay said that he had to go to work, my dad would take him aside, surreptitiously slip him some money, and say, "Jay, you're not going to work. You're going to do what you want to do, because you're going to be working hard the rest of your life." God bless my dad. He gave me that summer, and he said, "You just ride that motorcycle and don't get killed. That's the only rule I have. If you get killed, I'll ground your ass."

It was the perfect summer in almost every way. I was in love with a great girl, and every second Jay wasn't at work, we would ride around on our motorcycles. My cousin Dicky had bought a motorcycle, too, just so he could ride with us. He was with the U.S. Navy Reserve at that time, so he was home a lot and could run around and do all the crazy shit with us. None of us were bad kids, so most of the trouble we got into that summer was the kind that you could laugh off, but for all of the laughing we never forgot the sword of Damocles hanging over the train station in downtown Kansas City. We had an exact ship-out date, and as it started to approach, we began thinking more seriously about our choices. We would soon be leaving the comfort of our small hometown for unfamiliar and even hostile places in an unknown world for which we were barely prepared. Knowing this made us savor every moment that summer, soaking it all up with the vigor of boys who knew their boyhood was about to end.

CHAPTER 2

The House of Horrors

THERE WERE FIVE OF US from Van Horn High School on the train to boot camp and six other guys from Independence from two of the rival schools. We also picked up two other guys from Topeka along the way, and we all ended up in the same platoon. None of us knew how lucky we had it, but the long ride out to California gave us time to get to know each other and even question a few Marines who were going home on leave or just about to deploy to Vietnam. For some of the guys, it was their first taste of what awaited them at boot camp. For me, it just reinforced what I had already gleaned from pretty much every Marine I talked to back home. I knew it was going to be a genuine mind fuck and, even though I had read and thought about it a lot, I was in no way prepared for what was to come.

The train ride was basically like a high school field trip, but without teachers or chaperones. We got to unwind and had a lot of fun. The train staff treated us like gold, we ate like kings, and we all had these little rooms. Jay and I shared one, and that was actually quite special, but later, after an old girlfriend of his got on the train, I didn't get to spend much time in our room. She and Jay were too busy making memories before boot camp. We all hated him and envied the hell out of him but couldn't hold it against him. I ended up sleeping in the observation car, but had our roles been reversed, I sure as hell would have done what Jay did.

When we finally pulled in to Los Angeles's Union Station after three and a half days, we had to transfer to another train, which took us down to San Diego. It was also pretty luxurious, and we were lulled into a state of relaxation as the train barreled down the Pacific coast. A few hours later, when we arrived in San Diego, we got off the train and looked around for our contacts, but there wasn't anyone waiting for us in the station. We were slightly bewildered, surrounded by civilians and wondering what we were supposed to do. Then, out of the blue, these Marine NCOs walked right into the station and descended upon us, yelling at us and barking orders. We knew right then that we had entered a new world. The Marines reviewed our documents and quickly got us squared away. Then, instead of transferring us by bus to the recruit depot, they piled us all into the backs of military trucks.

As we drove through the heart of downtown San Diego, they told us, "You will not talk and you will not eye fuck the area." It was the first time I heard that phrase, "eye fuck," and I thought, *Ooh, I can't wait to tell my friends back home that one.* Of course, the first thing we did was start eye fucking the area, because it's San Diego and we're from Missouri, and I looked behind us and saw a Drill Instructor driving a convertible. He saw me looking at him, and I thought, *Oh, God. We're in for it.* But it turned out the Drill Instructor was just out on an errand and didn't give a shit what we were doing. We all locked up, stopped looking around, and didn't flinch from then on out.

The first thing they did after we arrived was shave our heads. If you had any moles, they told you to put your finger on them so they wouldn't cut them. Of course, as soon as a recruit put his finger on a mole, they would just bear down harder with the razor. When it was your turn, the barber would ask, "And how would you like your hair cut today?" And some of these guys were so dumb, they would actually say, "I'd like a little bit on top," which meant they would get fuckin' hammered. I'd had short haircuts most of my life because of my curly hair, but I'd never had it this short. It felt as if they took off two or three layers of skin.

Our heads shaved, we ran back outside at top speed, with the Drill Instructors screaming at us, and—as instructed—we placed our feet on the painted yellow footprints on the pavement, a hallowed Marine Corps tradition that signaled the beginning of our transformation from civilians to Marines. Jay and I stood there shoulder to shoulder at the front. We looked up and could see our reflections in the windows in front of us, at which point we both started to giggle, and this was not the thing to do as freshly shaved recruits. It was an incredible moment of transition. We were recruits, scared out of our wits, but still civilian enough to acknowledge the absurdity of how we looked. We wouldn't laugh again for many weeks, not until the very end of boot camp, when we finally began to relax.

The next thing they did was run us all into the receiving barracks, nicknamed the House of Horrors. As soon as we entered the building, they made us stand in front of these stalls in which they had placed cardboard boxes. "Everything you weren't born with," the Drill Instructors said, "goes in the box."

Beyond that, we were allowed to keep only our wallets. That was it. We couldn't hold on to rings or watches or anything else, which they made sure of, searching us for contraband, ordering us to strip naked and place our shirts, shoes, socks, Skivvies, and everything in our pockets in the boxes. Then they would go through individually and make sure we weren't trying to smuggle anything in. They found knives, cash, and all kinds of stuff; all the money was, of course, donated to the "recruit depot fund," which probably meant it went directly into their pockets. When everything was in place, they gave each of us a sticker, which we filled out with our addresses before flattening them onto the boxes, ready to be mailed home.

Then they ran us straight into the showers. You got sixty seconds, and we were all in there together at the same time. As it turned out, a number of the recruits, those who had gone to religious schools, had never been naked in the presence of other guys, and they stood out because they had these extra wide-eyed looks on their faces, expressing utter disbelief over what they had signed up for.

When the showers were cut off, everything started moving at double time. They ordered us to run, not walk, to the supply floor, where our clothing and other hygiene products—part of what was called our bucket issue—would be distributed and guys began slipping and tripping over each other. And when they collided and the bodies began piling up, it sounded like a heard of buffalo going over a cliff. The scene descended into chaos, flesh slamming against flesh. People were screaming obscenities, things I'd never heard before, and the overwhelming cacophony of voices quickly rose to become an unrelenting barrage of hatred and contempt. I got shoved forcefully into a wall, and then some guys fell on top of me. I was terrified and wondered if I was going to emerge from the pile alive, but then the voices of the Drill Instructors came raining down upon us, ordering us to get up and get into uniform.

We were issued one pair of trousers, one pair of Skivvies, one pair of socks, one Skivvy shirt, one utility jacket, and one yellow sweatshirt with a Marine Corps emblem, which thrilled the shit out of me. These days you can go to Walmart and buy a Marine Corps T-shirt, but in those days it wasn't so easy. I'd been dreaming about becoming a Marine, and the only item of clothing I owned that had an eagle, globe, and anchor on it was an old raggedy Marine utility jacket with none of its buttons that a girlfriend's father had given me. I was proud to own that jacket. Now I had my own sweatshirt and Marine utility covers, each featuring an eagle, globe, and anchor, the Marine Corps insignia. I was thrilled.

Before handing us our uniforms, the Drill Instructors drove us up a flight of stairs, where we were told to give them our trouser and head sizes. At the time, I had a twenty-eight-inch waist, but in the melee of all the guys screaming, I shouted out, "Thirty-six inches!" I had entered panic mode and lost all capacity for rational thought. There were Drill Instructors everywhere screaming at us, shoving us, and threatening to kill us, and everyone was yelling, "Run, run, run! You're too slow!" I have no doubt they knew, from just looking at me, my waist size was not thirty-six inches, but straightaway they threw me a pair of utility trousers, size 36. I didn't realize what had happened until I put them on, but then, all of a sudden, I found myself drowning in these trousers. We had each been issued a belt that was forty-four inches long, which we weren't allowed to trim. So there I was, wearing utility trousers that I had to fold over in order to get them to stay on, and they were barely held together by a forty-four-inch belt, the end of which was flopping around like an elephant's dick. I looked so ridiculous that one of the Drill Instructors yanked my cover down over my ears and told me that I looked like "ten pounds of shit in a five-pound bag."

When they told us to hold up our hands and let them know if something didn't fit, I was mortified, but even more so when I actually raised my hand and found myself in a complete world of shit for being the "stupidest motherfucker on earth." Was I the only child in my family to live, and were my parents cretins? they asked me. I didn't know what a cretin was, but I knew it couldn't be a compliment. So I got all of this extra abuse, while they brought guys in from other parts of the receiving barracks to get a good look at this "perfect example of what a maggot really is." They swore they were going to make a recruiting poster out of me. I was so fucking embarrassed.

Before anything else happened that night, we had to go for evening chow. They walked us outside, and because we weren't even official maggots yet, we weren't allowed to march. We were told to drag our feet and move to the nearest chow hall. Every Marine recruit in that chow hall, no matter if he'd been there a day or six weeks, stood ahead of us and was whispering insults at us, telling the instructors to make sure we got only about two bites of food. At one point, a Drill Instructor jumped up on the table and ran down it kicking our trays to the floor, screaming at us. The other recruits were terrorizing us, too, trying to humiliate us before we were taken back to the receiving barracks.

From that point on the abuse kept coming and it never let up. After being run around the House of Horrors for hours, screamed at from all sides and put through the paces, at one point we were made to stand in front of some stalls, and the

Drill Instructors left us there and were gone for a couple of hours, during which time, we were convinced, absolutely sure, that they were waiting outside the door, listening, waiting for us to make a sound. We were all so scared that no one said anything. We just stood there, fucking terrified out of our minds. And yet all that time nothing happened.

After seemingly endless hours of nonstop assault, just as we were about to collapse, we were marched out to the center racks and finally allowed to sleep for an hour or two. At first I was too scared to sleep, and I cried quietly in my rack. I was exactly where I had thought I wanted to be, and now all I wanted was to go home. I knew boot camp was going to be tough, but I had no idea how tough until that first night. I cried myself to sleep, and then they came in and threw a big shit can (or trash can) onto the concrete floor. Those who were actually still asleep were dragged out of their racks and thrown onto the deck. They were being slapped around, physically manhandled, by the Drill Instructors.

Boot camp was a very "hands-on" training back in the mid-1960s, and with the war on there weren't enough barracks for the recruits, many of whom ended up living in tents. We were lucky to have a roof over our heads. There were plenty of platoons out in "tent city" near the boundary to the San Diego airport that didn't have roofs. My platoon was in the 1105 series, which included four platoons, and each platoon had, as they said, seventy-five swinging dicks. We didn't end up with the same seventy-five guys we started with, but we did end up with the same number of recruits. People would fail tests or get injured and then would be dropped, and they would pick somebody else who had been dropped from another platoon, and he would end up in ours. Some unlucky guys would be dropped and picked up several times. The worst thing that could happen to you in boot camp was to be dropped and picked up, because then you were a known threat to any new platoon, which distrusted you immediately since you had obviously screwed up. The Drill Instructors didn't want you, because they thought you would lower their platoon's average, which they had worked so hard every day to achieve. A dropped recruit was one sorry fucker.

Early in boot camp, we learned that there were rules about speaking. Number one: you did not speak unless you were commanded to speak. Number two: the first word out of your mouth was always "sir." If they asked a question, and the answer was yes, you would say, "Sir, yes, sir." If you needed to speak, you would raise your hand and say, "Sir, Private Musgrave requests permission to speak." And the Drill Instructor would tell you to speak, if he felt like it, or to die or do any other weird thing he could come up with. But if he gave you permission to speak, you had to address him in a very specific way. The first thing you learned was to never use the word "I." We were not allowed to speak in the first person, only the third, as in "Sir, Private Musgrave requests permission to use the bathroom."

To which the Drill Instructor would reply, "Oh, no, no, no. Bathrooms are for civilians, Sailors, and queers. Marines go to the head."

Typically, you'd be told when to go to the head by numbers, but if you really had to go and couldn't wait, you'd say, "Sir, Private Musgrave requests permission to make an emergency head call, sir."

"Where the fuck you from, Private? Mars?" The DIs always found a way of drilling it into our heads that we had to say, "Platoon 1105."

"Sir, Private Musgrave, Platoon 1105, requests permission to speak to the Drill Instructor, sir."

"Speak."

"Sir, Private Musgrave, Platoon 1105, requests permission to make an emergency head call, sir."

And if they were really nasty, they would say, "Permission denied. And if you don't piss your pants, Private, I'll know you lied to me, and then I'm going to thrash you for lying."

Of course, if you did piss your pants, then you'd get thrashed for being "an animal." Soon you'd learn that you could never win and the world was not fair. Boot camp was where I first learned that lesson and where I quit believing in happy endings. I accepted that every encounter with a Drill Instructor was not going to end well and that I simply had to learn from my mistakes. All of the punishment and humiliation was designed to burn the memory of mistakes into our brains.

Making mistakes led me to learn the Marine Corps language. You didn't have eyeballs; you had "running lights." You didn't have a nose; you had a "snot locker." You didn't have a mouth; you had a "shit hole." Glasses were "portholes." Your head was a "gourd," "brain bucket," or "brain housing group." Your hands were "dick skinners." Your feet were "gunboats," or whatever your Drill Instructor wanted them to be. Underwear was called Skivvies. If you made the mistake of using the word "pants," you would soon hear, "Oh, no. Sailors and hookers wear pants. Marines wear trousers." As recruits, we wore these green utility trousers, white Keds, a yellow sweatshirt, and a green utility cover, which we were never allowed to wear squared. It had to be worn in a fucked-up fashion, for which we were called canaries. And that was the nicest thing we were ever called. "Go put on your canary suit for PT," or physical training, they would

*Six photo-booth photos of a friend and me in uniform
after graduating from boot camp.*

order. And that meant your running shorts, with your Marine-issued jockstrap, your Keds, and a Skivvies shirt. "Showering gear" consisted of a towel and flip-flops, which were called shower shoes.

In the Marine Corps, everything is nautical, because it's part of the Navy. We quickly learned that you don't stand on the floor. You stand on the "deck." You hang something not on the wall but on the "bulkhead." You look up not at the ceiling but at the "overhead." You don't walk through a door; you go through a "hatch." You don't walk down stairways; you go down "ladder wells." You don't go downstairs; you go "belowdecks." You had to learn this entirely new language and absorb this new culture by trial and error. The most common mode of learning was by physical training. Push-ups in the Marine Corps, it turned out, were different from push-ups in high school. And you didn't do jumping jacks; you did "side-straddle hops." Traditional bends and thrusts were unofficially called "bends and motherfuckers." Everything consisted of workout exercises. So one push-up was actually many push-ups, because they were all on the count of four, taking four times as long to complete as we slowly and laboriously lowered ourselves to the ground.

CHAPTER 3

Drill Instruction

IN THOSE DAYS, it seemed I was always making mistakes and then learning from them the hard way, often under the tutelage of Drill Instructors, who were all too happy to correct me whenever I strayed from the path. One of the biggest mistakes I made early was in taking the blame for someone else's mistake. We had just moved into our Quonset huts, and naturally we were all talking because we were excited and getting to know each other. Before we knew what had happened, a Drill Instructor suddenly charged into the hut, where close to a dozen of us were standing around. Whenever a Drill Instructor entered a hatch, the first person who saw him had to scream, "Attention!" Then we were supposed to run to our footlockers and stand at attention with the toes of our shoes touching the footlockers. The instructors would jump up on the footlockers and walk around, intimidating the shit out of us. As soon as the Drill Instructor entered our hut and heard the chatter, he asked who was talking. Of course, all of us were scared and no one said a word. And then he said, "If you don't tell me who's jackin' their fucking jaws in here, I'm going to murder all of you." So I did what I had always done at school, and at church camp, and at Boy Scout camp. I held up my hand and admitted that I had been talking, expecting that, as in the past, I would be commended for having the courage to admit it and would be told not to do it again. But that's not what happened.

The Drill Instructor was around six-four. Standing on my footlocker, he towered over me so that my head was at the height of his belt buckle. All of a sudden, without warning, he slapped me across the face with his open hand. I was stunned. I'd never been struck by an adult before except by my father, and never in my face. I had been in two fights in my life, both of which I had lost. He hit me so hard that I fell back against the double-decker racks. Then I was in even more trouble, because I had broken the position of attention.

I immediately scrambled back into position, and then he popped me again from the other side, and then from the other. Each time I moved, he hit me again. Then I started to flinch, which was an even bigger mistake. I was fucking petrified. After he was done making an example of me for talking and then leaving the position of attention whenever he hit me, he told me to stand up straight. Then he struck me forcefully in the throat. He definitely pulled his punch, because if he hadn't, he would probably have killed me. But it hurt all the same. It hurt like a son of a bitch. I gasped for air and could make only raspy noises as I struggled to breathe. He expected me to say that I understood, but I couldn't say anything, and I was even more terrified than before. At this point, he turned briskly, crossed the footlockers, and proceeded to manhandle this poor Mexican kid—the first I'd met in my life—because he, too, had held up his hand earlier, and likely regretted doing so right away when he saw how I was treated. He slapped the kid a few times and then let him be, having already made his point on my ass. As it turned out, this was all SOP, standard operating procedure, and it was one hell of a lesson for me. I think it was news to the rest of the platoon as well. I knew boot camp was going to be rough, and I even knew that we'd be slapped around and kicked in the shins and punched, because I had talked to Marines ahead of time. And I had thought, *This is going to be kinda cool. I'm going to take it like a man.* But when that Drill Instructor put his hands on me that first time, it was one of the most frightening things I had ever experienced. In boot camp, honest to God, I was the most afraid I've ever been in my life. I feared all Drill Instructors. I was afraid of some of the other recruits. And I was afraid to fail, because I had made such a big deal out of wanting to be a Marine my entire life. If I failed, it would have killed me. Boot camp wasn't anything like I thought it was going to be. It wasn't cool. It was terrifying and it hurt, and instead of rising up to become the tough guy that I thought I would be, I was just a teenage boy who wanted his mommy. Looking back on it now, I'm grateful for boot camp. If it hadn't been so hard, I wouldn't have survived the war.

A few days after that encounter, our platoon commander, who was a Korean War veteran, paced before us as we stood in tight formation. We knew he was our platoon commander from the moment we saw him, because he wore a black leather belt with a brass buckle on it. He gave us a welcome-aboard speech and let us know the rules of the recruit depot. The Drill Instructors were not allowed to smoke in front of us, he said, unless we were allowed to smoke. Drill instructors were not allowed to use profanity in our presence or curse at us. And Drill Instructors were never allowed to put their hands on recruits except to adjust their alignment, which later became a euphemism for getting thumped. If a Drill Instructor ever leaned over to you and said, "I'm going to adjust your alignment," you got ready to get hit. The platoon commander said all of these things, and I thought, *This is a beautiful day. These guys are going to find out what the other Drill Instructor did to me and this shit is going to stop now.*

The platoon commander pulled out a pack of cigarettes and lit one. At that very moment, I think my asshole slammed shut. And there were probably seventy-four other guys thinking the same thing. In the instant that he lit that cigarette, the platoon commander made all too clear that while the rules in his speech might have been the rules at headquarters, down here he was a god who didn't care about the official rules and could do whatever he wished. Then he proceeded to cuss. He told us that "fuck" was a Marine Corps–issued word that civilians were allowed to use. It was not just a word. It was an integral part of other words, like "out-fucking-standing" and "get-the-fuck-out-of-here." If a word had two syllables, in the Marine Corps it would end up having three. As he cursed, he moved down the line and slapped every single one of us, or punched us in the stomach. "This is the way it's going to work," he said. "And none of you will ever say a word to anyone outside this platoon about what goes on in this platoon."

Later, in Vietnam, the platoon commander's speech came back to me often, because you never talked candidly to anyone who was "non-unit personnel." For example, if you encountered a Marine who was not part of your unit, you would never tell him what your unit did in the field. If a reporter approached you and started asking questions, you would never tell him what your unit really did, because you might end up sending people to jail. As far as anyone was concerned, the rules we followed were the rules of the Geneva Convention. But as with boot camp, the bush had its own set of rules. The enemy set them, and we reacted to them. Boot camp was like that, too. We learned at the recruit depot that there was only one world, the world of Platoon 1105, and you wouldn't tell a Drill Instructor from another platoon about your world, even if he got in your face and demanded it. This became abundantly clear to me during an unfortunate encounter with a Drill Instructor at company headquarters.

Every day, each platoon would assign two recruits to hang out at the company headquarters. The first thing a company runner does is set up the office for the platoon commanders' briefing in the morning. So, one day, during the seventh or eighth week, while serving in this capacity, I was inside company headquarters getting the coffee ready, while a large group of Drill Instructors and platoon commanders filed into the room. As they entered, one of them saw me and asked me where I was from.

"Sir, Private Musgrave, Platoon 1105," I replied.

Looking me up and down, he said, "Platoon 1105. I see. So you're Erxleben's turd," referring to my Drill Instructor, Staff Sergeant Erxleben. "Well, has Erxleben ever done this?" he asked as he stomped down on my foot with full force. It hurt, but I tried not to show it.

"Sir, no, sir," I said.

He kicked me in the shin. "Did he ever do that?"

"Sir, no, sir."

He punched me in the stomach.

"Sir, no, sir."

"He ever make you do the chicken?"

Nobody ever wanted to do the chicken, when the Drill Instructor would take his fingers—his index and middle—and his thumb, grab your larynx, and squeeze as hard as he could.

And, as your tongue shot forth from your mouth under the pressure of his grip, up from the depths of your throat would come the sounds of a chicken: "Gah, gah, gah!" And that is what they called doing the chicken.

"Erxleben ever make you do the chicken?" he repeated as he grabbed me by the throat and made me "Gah, gah, gah" a few times. I managed to force out an answer through my constricted airway: "Sir, no, sir!" By that point, I'd been at boot camp long enough to know that this was a test and it would hopefully soon be over. "All right," he said, "you're a good turd. Get out of here." Then he turned to Erxleben and said, "That turd over there is a good turd," which made me say a prayer of thanks to God. I thought it was over and breathed a sigh of relief as soon as I was out of sight, but my troubles that day had only just begun.

I knew better than to fall for it, but for some reason later that afternoon I got caught off guard by my platoon commander when he asked me a question in front of another platoon commander. It was a simple question, and I delivered a clear and simple answer. But then he switched gears and tripped me up by saying something I hadn't expected, and I committed the ultimate sin.

"But, sir . . . you . . . ," I said, realizing my error as it escaped from my lips. *Oh, I am such a dumb fucking idiot,* I thought, because a recruit never referred to a Drill Instructor with the second-person pronoun. A ewe is a female sheep.

"Oh, I'm a ewe?" the platoon commander said. "So you like me, Private? Do you want to FUCK me, Private?"

"Sir, no, sir."

"You don't want to fuck me?"

"Sir, no, sir."

"Oh, I'm not good enough for you, am I?"

It was just one of those situations—all too common in boot camp—in which everything I said was wrong. The absolute worst thing you could do is embarrass your Drill Instructor or platoon commander in front of another Drill Instructor, and I had done just that. I had called him a female sheep in front of another platoon commander, who—to make matters worse—happened to be his rival.

So he went and got his so-called medicine, a big bottle of Tabasco sauce with a white piece of paper wrapped around it that said, "EWE MEDICINE."

"Tip your head back, open your mouth, and stick out your tongue," he commanded. "You got to take your medicine." He shook about half the bottle into my mouth and then made me hold it for more than a minute. Then he said, "Swallow," and I swallowed. *Jesus,* I thought, *thank God that's over.* The Tabasco was burning my throat, and I could feel it searing the lining of my stomach. "Tilt back your head," he said, and he made me down that whole son of a bitch, all because I had embarrassed him in front of this guy. Then he made me do PT, sweating and grunting at their feet, before letting me go.

As soon as I was dismissed from company runner duty, I sprinted down to the wash racks, where we did our laundry with lava soap and hand brushes in large concrete basins. I opened up a faucet and drank about a gallon of water to get the fire out of my mouth and stomach. Of course, I never made that mistake again. That was the way you learned lessons in boot camp, and that was the world in which we lived. I didn't smoke then or now, but in boot camp smoking was the only reward that was allowed. The DIs would announce in naval parlance that the "smoking lamp" was lit for one cigarette. While they smoked, the nonsmokers did PT. Skip started smoking just so he wouldn't have to do extra PT, and he still smokes like a chimney today.

The finest Drill Instructor we had at the recruit depot was an African American sergeant named Gardner. Though he could be hard on recruits, and my interactions with him weren't always the happiest experiences, my respect for him never wavered. Our other junior Drill Instructor, the one who thumped me that first time, was a big guy. He was illiterate, and if there hadn't been a war on, he never would have made it through Drill Instructor school, because he couldn't even read orders to us. And the son of a bitch didn't have any rhythm either, so he couldn't even call cadence. We looked like a Busby Berkeley dance routine out there, trying to keep up with him, which meant that he'd get really angry and thrash us until we threw up or passed out. We had very little respect for him. But we all looked up to Sergeant Gardner. He was a real pro and had our best interests in mind. By being tough on us, he was trying to prepare us for battle. Our platoon commander was just a sadistic son of a bitch who didn't care if we lived or died.

One day, about two or three weeks into boot camp, while Gardner was busy squaring us away, he started dealing with one recruit, whose name escapes me. Gardner wasn't striking him or anything; he was just getting his alignment sorted out, when this guy yelled, "Take your dirty nigger hands off me!" We all thought, *Holy shit, you can't say that to a Drill Instructor.* We knew Gardner was going to kill this motherfucker.

Gardner stepped back. "What did you say, Private?" he asked.

"I said take your dirty nigger hands off me!" the recruit replied. "And if you touch me again, I'm going to kill you."

We were all floored. Out of seventy-five of us in that platoon, there were only two black recruits. There were several Hispanics, but most of us were just white kids from the middle of

America. Gardner, who could have gotten away with thumping the shit out of this guy right there, stepped closer to him.

"You want to take a shot at me?" Gardner asked.

"Yeah, I'll kick your ass."

So Gardner commanded us to all stand at attention, while he stepped over between the Quonset huts with the guy. I remember seeing him take off his "smoky-brown round," strip his blouse, and take off his pistol belt. Removing his blouse was like removing his rank; they were just two guys. Taking off his pistol belt said that he was not on official duty. Then he let this shithead take the first shot. The kid took a swing at him, and then Gardner beat the living shit out of him, and we were all wide-eyed and motivated, watching him pound this gob of spit, beating him down. Finally, Gardner said, "All right. That's it. Get up, get your shit together, and get out of here." And then this guy had the audacity to go back and tell the Navy doctor that Gardner had beaten him mercilessly, though he had done nothing wrong.

The worst word a Drill Instructor could hear was "maltreatment." If he was accused and convicted of it, he would be court-martialed. A group from the Naval Criminal Investigative Service came and interviewed all of us about Gardner, who had been accused of maltreatment. We'd already been advised by our Drill Instructors on how to answer the questions so they wouldn't be misinterpreted by the investigators, and we all spoke in favor of Gardner and told them how the recruit had been way out of line and how Gardner had let the guy take the first shot. Ultimately, Sergeant Gardner was acquitted of the charge of maltreatment, but he was taken off the drill field and given orders to go to WestPac, or the western Pacific, which meant Vietnam.

It wasn't until after the Vietnam Veterans Memorial had

been built, while leafing through a directory to the wall, that I found out what happened to Sergeant Gardner. I had been going through my boot camp annual to figure out how many guys from my platoon had been killed in the war, when I stumbled across his name. It turned out that Sergeant Gardner had arrived in Vietnam and had been killed in action before we arrived. That remarkable noncommissioned officer—such an outstanding Marine—had been murdered by that cowardly, racist gob of spit who didn't have the fortitude to take his licking like a man. He might as well have walked up behind Gardner and shot him in the back of the head. It broke my heart when I saw his name in that book. He died because of bigotry at the hands of that recruit and at the hands of the command. What infuriated us was that Sergeant Gardner, while being acquitted of the charge of maltreatment, was still removed from the drill field and given orders to Nam as if he were guilty. I don't believe it was based on race. It boiled down to the command not having the guts to back up their NCOs. NCOs are the backbone of the Corps, and Drill Instructors are the elite of the NCOs. That act had a negative effect on our platoon, on me, and led to his death. It didn't diminish my love for the Corps. It just made it clear that officers couldn't be trusted.

One day during the first week of boot camp, when we were taking our academic tests, the Drill Instructors showed us a chart of MOSs, Military Occupational Specialties, or job descriptions. One of the DIs said, "When you complete this form, at the top right-hand corner, write in the three MOS fields that you would like to be considered for." Well, that was a no-brainer for me. I put 0300, 0300, and 0300. Infantry, infantry, and infantry. I didn't join the Marine Corps to drive a truck. I didn't join to type at a desk. And I certainly didn't join to play in the Marine Corps band. So I didn't tell them that I could play a musical instrument. I joined the Marine Corps to be the ultimate Marine. The heart and soul of the Corps is the rifleman. They called riflemen the hub of the wheel. Everyone else was considered spokes that supported the hub. From that day forward, for the rest of boot camp, I was terrified I was going to end up a cook. I lived in fear that I would be dropped, because I'd never been an athlete and wasn't nearly as fit as some of the other recruits. But during boot camp I realized what the Scouts had done for me, with all the swimming, physical activity, and endurance tests. At boot camp, I discovered I could do things that I never thought possible.

As a child, I learned about the draft as soon as I was old enough to learn about duty and obligation. I knew that I owed my country two years of military service, and the only choice I had in the matter was to select the branch of service. Of course, if there hadn't been a draft, most of my buddies wouldn't have joined the Marine Corps. The reason they joined was to exercise what little choice they had. Many came from families with fathers and grandfathers who had served in the Corps. Others simply felt that the training they got in the Corps would give them a better chance of returning home alive. They preferred the Corps to the other services, but given a choice, they would have preferred to stay home with their girlfriends, work a shit job stacking groceries, and maybe earn enough money to buy a car. They would have preferred to grow up slowly, learn from their mistakes, and live regular lives. To me, that was doom. I wanted a life of adventure and challenge. But there are fifty-eight thousand names engraved in black marble in Washing-

The first photo I sent my folks of me in my "greens"
to show how tough I was now! San Diego, California, 1966.

ton, D.C., commemorating the sacrifices of young men who, because of the draft, had entered the war against their wishes, because of the color of their skin, the neighborhoods they came from, or the fact that they couldn't afford to go to college. When I joined the Corps, I was exactly where I wanted to be, and yet I was still terrified and secretly hoping they were going to discover that I had some strange disease that would send me home with honor. Those first few hellish weeks of boot camp, I kept praying, *Gimme something, God. Visit me with sickness,* but eventually, as I got stronger, and the platoon got better and more resilient, I stopped having these thoughts and began to take pride in what was starting to happen to us.

The day it really came together for the platoon, we were out on the grinder, the big asphalt parking lot where we drilled. On this hot summer day—it was like walking on a skillet over a fire—we were doing some type of drill, and the Drill Instructors were yelling at us, "One heel, one heel. I want to hear one heel strike the ground!" This meant we shouldn't sound like a centipede, with more than a hundred legs moving at different times, we needed to move our feet in unison. To this point, we still hadn't found our rhythm, which isn't something that can be taught. It's something intuitive, like a sixth sense; you can't understand until it happens.

We were performing our manual arms on the march, slapping our M14s. They had nice hardwood stocks. To prepare us for slapping the stocks of our rifles, the DIs had us on our hands and knees slapping the grinder as hard as we could, until our hands were rough and tight. They yelled, "One hand, one hand, one heel!" Then, unexpectedly, the training began to take hold and everything fell into place. Suddenly, as we marched, our feet moved in unison, and for the first time we were a real platoon. We instantly knew that we had risen above the level of "maggots and turds." We were Marine recruits, and if they didn't kill us in the process, we were going to make it to the other side. In that moment, a whole new attitude took hold of us. Suddenly we were standing up straighter, our shoulders squared, our heads high, our eyes fixed in a permanent Clint Eastwood squint. It's hard to describe the feeling, a mixture of pride and profound relief, of finally belonging to a platoon and knowing that no matter what awaited us in Southeast Asia, we were now part of the greatest and most iconic fighting force the world has ever seen. Marines aren't taught to march in a straight line. Marines move with purpose, and that is what we started to do that hot summer day on the meat grinder. Although our transformation was far from complete, it had begun.

CHAPTER 4

Finishing School

*My platoon group. I'm third from the left in the second row
from the top. San Diego, 1966.*

GRADUATION IN THE MARINE CORPS is designed to make you feel like a million bucks. It's an extraordinary experience. It's the first time you're called a Marine by your battalion commander, and earning that title changes your life forever. Also, you know that what you've learned at the recruit depot will stay with you for the rest of your days. Even guys who were mediocre recruits and shitty Marines acquired a code that guided their choices and gave them the determination and will to persevere during the darkest of times. For me, graduation was a total rebirth; an entirely new John Musgrave came out of there, a confident, physically aggressive Marine. I looked and felt different. I had self-respect for the first time in my life. It was a big fucking moment. Nowadays, they let Marines go home and be with their folks on graduation day, but we had roughly four hours on base with everybody to celebrate, and then we were sent back to the Quonset huts with our Drill Instructors, who took us straight to the sandpits, where we were made to do physical training in ankle-deep sand, to show us that in spite of what we had accomplished, we were still turds in their eyes. Nevertheless, the whole time in the pits we were laughing, because we were Marines and there wasn't anything they could do to us now. It was totally liberating.

The next morning, we lined up and boarded buses that took us to Camp Pendleton, about an hour north of San Diego on the California Pacific coast, where we began learning how to be professional killers and building bonds with a whole new group of friends that would last a lifetime. MCRD San Diego had been where we were initiated and indoctrinated. Camp Pendleton was our finishing school, where we learned our trade. All 299 guys in the 1105 series arrived in those buses at Camp Pendleton for four weeks of infantry training, and then those of us who received an infantry MOS would be staying another four weeks. A lot of the guys who were important to me, many of whom were later killed in the war and now occupy the "honor wall" of photos in my home in Kansas, I met at Camp Pendleton after graduating from boot camp. Our bond and friendship, however brief, made a deep and indelible imprint on my life, and I am who I am now because of them.

The buses took us to the school of infantry, where we were

Seven photo-booth photos of me in uniform at my first shore liberty.

assigned to Mike Company, nicknamed Running Mike, because it was known for running trainees into the ground. That said, we were definitely treated with more respect, and in the evenings guys brought out little transistor radios and Instamatic cameras. We weren't allowed to listen to music during boot camp, and I was jonesing for some good rock and roll. I was a Beach Boys fanatic, and when I finally heard "Good Vibrations" in one of the Quonset huts in the barracks, after having run up and down Old Smokey, also known as Mount Motherfucker because of its extreme height, all day, it was just about the best sound in the world.

Because of the war, there weren't enough M14s to go around. We had them in boot camp, but at ITR, Infantry Training Regiment, we were issued M1 Garands, .30-caliber semiautomatic rifles that had been standard issue to troops during World War II and the Korean War. When we got to Vietnam, we were issued the same equipment that was used during the 1930s, but we didn't mind, because we looked like our heroes from World War II and Korea. The web gear that we wore—packs, belts, straps, canteen covers, ammunition pouches, and so on—had all been designed more than thirty years prior and was called 782 gear. I was the automatic rifleman in my squad, and when we went through Automatic Rifleman training, I got to carry a Browning Automatic Rifle, also known as the BAR, which was just about the sexiest weapon of the previous two wars. It was one heavy motherfucker, but I looked like such a badass carrying it that I thought I was Chesty Puller (the most decorated Marine in American history). I also had an assistant automatic rifleman whose job was to carry my extra magazines. Even when we were just carrying the M1s, we still had to hold an extra roll, because we had to pretend we were carrying whatever weapon we were supposed to be carrying.

The first night, we were all standing in alphabetical order in the Mike Company area, a group of Quonset huts with its own little mini-grinder, and this redheaded smart-ass city guy with a thick accent named Jim Murray asks me my name. It seems as if 80 percent of the Marine Corps were from Texas or Chicago, so this guy's Chicago accent wasn't so out of place. I told him my name, and he said, "Moooozzz-grave." And this was pretty unfortunate, because from that moment on my name had a z in it. Right away, he started dickin' with me, and I realized after a few minutes that he was actually the funniest motherfucker I had met since Jay, and I just needed to maneuver around all the horseshit he was throwing at me so that we could be friends.

Jim, who went by the nickname Moose, was in a gang called the Turfers. They wore white Levi's and even had their own song, which he happily sang for me. He was not much of a singer, but he would always sing it to me. He called it a gang, but I suspect it was just his high school buddies. We got to jacking with each other and trading barbs, so much so that we both burst out laughing and got busted by one of our troop leaders— no longer at this point called Drill Instructors—who gave us the dreaded "Get down and give me fifty." So we both hit the deck and started putting out fifty push-ups, but even then we kept fucking with each other, saying things like "If you can't finish them, sweetheart, I'll finish them for you." We would say the rudest things we could think of, all the while barely able to catch our breath as we were doing the push-ups. We were laughing so hard that we both nearly passed out. This was the beginning of a beautiful friendship. We racked together and stood beside each other every day for the next two months. We were pretty much inseparable.

Moose was legitimately tough, a genuine badass, and I never really understood why he seemed to feel so lucky to have me as a friend, but I sure felt lucky to be friends with him. He made ITR completely bearable, as did another guy in our squad named Gordon Miller. Moose was the fire team leader, and

Gordy was my A-gunner. Gordy was everything I wanted to be. He was a southerner, transplanted from North Carolina to Indiana, and he oozed southern charm. I was a northern Missouri bushwhacker, but I loved Gordy and became close with his family. His sister wrote to me all through training and then through Vietnam, and we ended up corresponding for years afterward. He was one of the most genuine people I've ever met. We were brothers—Gordy, Moose, and I, and another guy named Bill Petrossi—the closest of friends.

I met Bill at ITR during rifleman training. The training consisted of four weeks of running back and forth to classes, which were held miles apart, and we'd never travel by road. We'd crawl and climb our way through Camp Pendleton, a very hilly Southern California terrain, crisscross through streams, and then hump as hard as we could up steep inclines to make it to class on time. Then we'd spend all day firing automatic rifles, rocket launchers, grenade launchers, and flamethrowers, because every Marine in the infantry had to be able to pick up any other weapon and utilize it. We threw hand grenades, and I learned to love them. We attended prisoner of war class and learned how to escape captivity by navigating the constellation Orion at night. We learned radio skills. And we learned how to abandon ship, jumping off huge towers without getting hurt.

We also learned drown proofing, a process by which a person can remain alive in the water for hours. You bend your waist, relax your shoulders, and float, keeping your face submerged in the water. Every ten to twelve seconds you lift your face above the water, take a breath, then turn your face back into the water, and relax. If done properly, with minimal movement, your body will continue floating, just below the level of the water, while you gently bob up and down. Using this technique, a person can remain alive in the water for hours, even days, without any floatation gear. For some reason, even though I had been a lifeguard and a swimming instructor, I failed drown proofing the first time I took it. I was very confident in the water, but for some reason—as I soon discovered—I could not float. In order to graduate as a "second-class swimmer," I had to swim around an Olympic-size pool. Had I not been able to do that, I might not have made it through infantry training to deploy with my friends. I'm not saying the Marine Corps lowered their standards just so I could ship out to Vietnam, but I counted my lucky stars that I was being sent to a land war.

We also got our first liberties at ITR. On Saturday mornings, we would have to get into uniform for a Class A inspection. If you were a trainee and you passed your inspection, you got liberty aboard, which meant you couldn't leave the base. Later, we got liberty ashore, which meant off base. If something was out of place or scuffed, and your uniform wasn't completely squared away, you would fail the inspection, and you wouldn't receive your liberty card. If you failed your rifle inspection, because it hadn't been properly cleaned or assembled, you might get the M1 thumb, which was when the instructors would stick your thumb in the chamber of your weapon and then let the bolt slam home on it. I never failed a rifle inspection at any point during my time in the Marine Corps, and I'm pretty proud of that. But I saw other guys fumble their rifle inspections and then get their thumbs busted. They learned the hard way that although we were done with boot camp, we were still at the bottom of the hill, and the shit always rolled downhill.

On my first liberty ashore, I planned to travel down to San Diego to visit some cousins of my parents whom I called Uncle Marvin and Aunt Edna. They were wonderful people. Uncle

Marvin had the world's second-largest pencil collection, which had been written up in newspapers and books. He was a gentle giant—somewhere around six six—so large that you could roll quarters through his ring, which he loved showing people. On my way to see Uncle Marvin and Aunt Edna, I ran into some guys from ITR who were going to a bar. They told me to come along, so I called Uncle Marvin and told him that I wasn't going to be released that day and that I would call them in the morning.

At this point, I still looked about twelve, maybe fifteen, and pretending to be a Marine. There was no way anybody was going to give me beer. Plus, I was in uniform, so everyone I met would know I was a trainee. San Diego has always been a Navy town, and there were squids (or Sailors) everywhere. We ducked into a bar, and naturally it was filled with them. You could tell who the Marines in civilian clothing were, because they all had high and tights, that unmistakable Marine Corps haircut featuring about an inch of hair on top and closely shaved sidewalls. I sat down at the bar and ordered a Coke, while my buddies tried hitting on a couple of the barmaids. They weren't getting anywhere, but they were certainly having fun trying. I had a girlfriend back home, and as a Christian I didn't believe in drinking; I had vowed to my parents that I would never drink, a promise I kept until I came home from the war.

So there I was, nursing my Coke, when suddenly I heard a commotion over by the dance floor. I looked over, saw a Sailor arguing with a guy in civilian clothes with a high and tight, and I knew this had the potential to end badly. The Sailor had crossed a line, referring to the Marine by a favorite Navy insult, a "seagoing bellhop." The Marine had immediately shot back with the standard rejoinder, "The only bell I hopped was your mother," and simultaneously he picked up a pitcher of beer and hit the squid square in the side of the head with it, knowing that when he uttered those words, there was going to be a fight. I stood there with my jaw open, in total shock, when I heard him yell, "Marines, I'm in trouble!" at which point this thing kicked in, deep within the DNA of every Marine in the room. We were all honor bound by a code that stretched back to the 1700s to protect that Marine.

I was by no means a brawler, but I was relatively confident in my hand-to-hand combat skills, because I had just been trained at the recruit depot. There was a squid at the other end of the bar from me, and he wasn't very big. So I zeroed in on this guy, who seemed like someone I could handle, and started advancing on him. As I approached him, he jumped off his bar stool and bent over, and I squared off as if we were going to box. When he bent over, I didn't know what to think. *Maybe he's surrendering?* was something that foolishly crossed my mind. But then he pulled off his blue scarf and swung it around as fast as he could, snapping it right up against the bridge of my nose. What I didn't know at the time, and my cousin who had served in the Navy had to explain to me later, was that the guy had a roll of dimes sewn into his neckerchief. And when that roll of dimes struck my nose, my nose fractured, and the blow sent me reeling backward. He hit me so hard I went cross-eyed. That had never happened before. I couldn't even see him, let alone hit him. I'd never been hit that hard in the nose. It radiated its own special, all-encompassing pain, kind of like getting kicked in the nuts. It was so painful that I saw flashes of light and color.

Unfortunately, this guy wasn't done with me. He kept swinging that roll, striking me on the top and sides of my head, beating the ever-living shit out of me, until my buddies came over and dragged me out of the bar. As they pulled me into the street,

I covered my face and my head with my hands, trying not to bleed on my greens. I remember thinking that I couldn't get blood on my uniform on my first liberty ashore. Blood was gushing through my hands, but I was relieved that it was finally over.

The funny thing was that I hadn't even stretched out my arm to punch the guy. I never committed or made contact. All I possessed in that fight was an abundance of overconfidence, and I got one hell of an education. The first thing I should have known when I squared off with the guy was there ain't nothing fair in a bar fight. The Marine hit the squid with a glass pitcher, not a fist. And my opponent struck me with a roll of dimes. He wasn't about to square off and box. All told, the fight probably lasted only thirty seconds before my world turned to tunnel vision and flashes of light, but those thirty seconds made me not want to get into any more fights for the rest of my life.

In the end, I returned from liberty on Sunday night with two black eyes and had to tell everybody the story of getting my ass handed to me by a fucking squid. So everyone in the platoon kept hammering me for at least a week, that is, until they moved on to someone else who had done something equally dumb, if not worse. For a while, though, I was the butt of every joke. Moose and Gordy were my defenders. They wouldn't beat a broken man, but everybody else did. This also garnered me the attention of some other guys in the platoon and actually made me a lot of friends. It's hard to explain, but things like that would make you the center of attention for a week or so, and while it was embarrassing as hell, it would usually work out for the best, that is if you didn't take it too seriously, and I didn't. In fact, I spent a lot of time laughing at myself, too, which is maybe what earned me those extra friends.

Uncle Marvin and Aunt Edna had fussed over me a lot when

I showed up Sunday morning with my face bruised, wads of cotton stuck up my nose, and two swollen eyes. I tried to stand up tall and proud in my uniform but must have been a pathetic sight. They were kind enough to wait until my next liberty to send pictures home to my parents. From that point on, every weekend when I went on liberty, I didn't go hang out with the guys anymore, but headed straight for Marvin and Edna's, where I would stay home, eat good food, listen to records on my uncle's stereo system, and spend time with my cousins, which was all a welcome break from the chaos and grind of infantry training.

At ITR we got to feel like real Marines preparing to go to war, and we were getting pretty pumped because a real war awaited us on the other side of the ocean. It wasn't just a slim possibility or some distant dream. We had received our orders in boot camp. The night before graduation, when my orders were read, I felt an overwhelming sense of calm pass over me. The Drill Instructor read out our MOSs, our training assignments, and our next armament duty stations, and when he came to me, as with most of the other guys in the platoon, he said, "0300 Infantry," and then, "WestPac," which was the western Pacific theater of operations—in other words, Vietnam. That night I got my wish. Everyone in ITR had WestPac orders, which is why we took infantry training so seriously. Our lives and those of people we loved would depend on it.

ITR gave me basic infantry training, but it also gave me a big group of friends. Gordy and I always wanted to be Marines. We believed in the brotherhood of warriors and were dyed-in-the-wool romantics about war. Moose was much more of a realist, and so was Billy. They were both far more mature. But Gordy and I were damn near giggling with excitement every time we

Me at Camp Pendleton in November 1966 at age eighteen.

talked about how we were going to be on the field of honor. Both of us were history buffs, but we weren't so arrogant as to think that we were going to be writing history; we just believed that our blood would be the ink in the pen, and that was enough for us. So every day at ITR was a rehearsal for war, and some days we even participated in war games and actually got to play war.

Right after ITR was BITS, Basic Infantry Training School. Our group went to Camp Horno, at Camp Pendleton, where the Recon School was located. BITS was supposed to last four weeks, but because of the mounting casualties in Vietnam it was compressed into two. Our training was no less rigorous. We just did it in half the time. BITS training was a refinement of the infantry tactics we had been introduced to in ITR. Because of the condensed schedule, we trained all day every day, from reveille to taps, with no breaks and no liberties in the evenings, even on board, and no weekend liberties either. BITS was just hammer and tongs for two solid weeks, extremely intense training. All of my buddies were there, and some of us had been together from the day we arrived at the recruit depot right until then, so we really got to know each other well. Although we might not all have traveled the same route, we all pretty much arrived in Vietnam at the same time, due to our training cycles.

Moose Murray had fractured his ankle at ITR, and they allowed us to miss only three training days before we'd be dropped. If you were dropped, you'd be taken out of the unit until your injury healed, picked up by the next training cycle. It meant leaving all of your friends and having to serve with strangers. None of us wanted to be dropped. So after three days, he convinced our instructors that he was all right and he came back to Mike Company to run through the hills of Camp Pendleton with a fractured ankle. Moose took me aside and made me promise I'd never let him drop out. And I said, "I don't know if you want me to promise that, because I'll do it." And he said, "I know you will. That's why I'm asking." So I agreed, and that meant that I had to be a bastard to him on a number of occasions, because he was hurt really bad, but he never dropped out. I would help him put his boot on, and he would cinch it as tightly as he could, and then we ran those damn hills all night for six more weeks. He tried to drop out a few times, but only a few, because the pain was overwhelming. I certainly couldn't have done what he did. It was hard to stand by and watch him go through it, but I had made a promise not to let him quit. So I'd grab him and push him and shove him and cuss at him, and then I'd ask him to forgive me, and then I'd cuss at him some more. In the end, he made it all the way through, and he turned out to be an outstanding Marine, as well as one of my closest friends. Moose was decorated in Vietnam and made sergeant before he got out of the Corps to return to Chicago to start his life outside the military.

When we graduated from BITS on December 22, we all felt especially lucky the training had been only two weeks, because it meant we would get to go home for Christmas and New Year's. The night before we left, they read our orders out to us. Of course, I already knew mine. I was going to Vietnam, and so was almost everyone else, except, as it turned out, for Moose. When they got to him, they read out, to our great shock and dismay, "Second Marine Division, Camp Lejeune, North Carolina." We were all taken aback. Moose's face turned ashen and white, and he looked as if he had just been read a death sentence. He simply couldn't believe he wasn't going to be coming with us. I couldn't believe it either, because Moose and I had spent a lot of time planning how we were going to go over there and kick some ass. I figured if Moose was with me, I could pull it off, and when we separated the next day, we both were wiping away tears, afraid that we'd never see each other again. The intensity of the time we'd spent together training had forged an indelible bond between us. It was unthinkable that we wouldn't be going to war together, and I was consumed by an immense feeling of loss.

When we graduated from BITS, the one last way for the instructors to stick it to us was with a final haircut. Many of us were growing our hair, and some even had enough on their heads to go home on leave and not look like skinned grapes or cue balls. But, sure enough, two days before we went home, they marched us down to the barbershop. We all thought, *No sweat. We'll get a touch-up and will be out looking sharp in our uniforms in no time.* Instead, they shaved our heads down to the skin, and, boy, were we pissed about it. Each of us was proud of the inch of hair he had grown over those six weeks. We were just fucking smoked. At the end of the day, though, we had to swallow our pride and accept that the Marine Corps had its ways.

My parents had purchased a ticket home for Christmas for me. I packed my bag and got ready to go. Though I was excited to see my folks and sleep in my own bed, I was a little apprehensive about returning because my girlfriend, Karen, had written me a Dear John letter while I was away. When it arrived, during ITR, I had been thrilled to receive a letter from her. I tore open the envelope and started reading it right away. Thank goodness Moose was with me at the time, because he saw my face fall and immediately knew what had happened. I took off, sprinted down to the Quonset hut, and ran into the head, where I crumpled up and started bawling. Jim followed me into the head, put his arms around me, and softly said, "Man, it's all right. It's her loss." I was so hurt and pissed that all I could do was tell him all the mean shit I was going to say in the letter back to her. With a calm, steady voice, Jim cautioned me not to do it. "Don't even answer the letter," he said. "She's just waiting for a letter from you saying how hurt and pissed you are. Don't let her get it. Trust me. Don't answer, and let her wonder what the hell is going on." Of course, Jim was right. In the silence of my not responding, Karen started writing me "forgive me" letters while I was in BITS, and when I finally came home, by the first Sunday at church, we were back together.

She was a beautiful young woman whom I had known from church and church camp. She was younger than I and was still in high school when I went away to become a Marine. During that time, naturally, she started getting asked out by jocks and "cool guys" and decided that she shouldn't have to wait for me when these other boys wanted to take her out and spend money on her. I think her father also encouraged her to move on, because he didn't like me. Her girlfriends were telling her she was too young to be spending her high school years, when she could be having fun, waiting for an enlisted Marine to come home. All the same, we got back together when I came back for Christmas, and we were in love. On Christmas Eve, I asked her to marry me, and she said yes. We started making plans for when I got out, and we even chose a name for our first kid.

We were supposed to get thirty days pre-embarkation leave, but were given only eighteen. When I first got back, I went straight to my old high school to show off the new me. My brother said that when I walked in the door, he thought I might have to angle sideways just to get my shoulders through the frame. He simply couldn't believe how different I looked. Of course, I couldn't see what he saw, because the changes had been gradual. I just knew that I had put on some weight and had filled out a bit.

Spending time back in the civilian world only reinforced how little it appealed to me. I had been in the Marine Corps for only about six months, and yet I looked at what the civilians I encountered were doing as bullshit. Through the Corps, I had found meaning and pride and had gained respect for myself and for my buddies. I had made some of the best friends in the world, and I got to shoot real guns and throw hand grenades. I was still just a kid, no more mature than when I enlisted, but I shed my civilian identity like a snakeskin. This was the new John Musgrave. There would be no more of that little boy getting pushed around. There would be no more taking orders from a bully of a manager whom I did not respect, at some minimum wage job. Even at the lowest moments of my training, when I was treated like shit by the Drill Instructors, I still held them in utmost respect and had true reverence for what they had done to attain their positions. During boot camp and infantry training, I had been surrounded by my heroes. And once I had a glimpse of that world, I took off my rearview mirror and threw it in a ditch, because I never wanted to look back upon my civilian life, except to think about family and friends.

During leave, I didn't drink or go out partying. Instead, I loved going to church with my mom, dad, and grandma, who lived next door to us. She only came up to below my shoulder, but she seemed tall with pride as she stood next to me in my greens at church, my mother on one side and she on the other, with our arms locked as we sang hymns. All of the people at that church had known me since I was four, so it felt even more like a community than my high school. It was a huge part of my identity. To walk into that church was to walk into my life and into a loving, supportive group of people who were all proud of my service.

On Christmas Eve, I had a special night with my parents, my grandmother, my girlfriend, Karen, and Butch and his wife, Gloria. We all gathered around the tree, and I was given things my family thought I'd be able to use while I was in the Corps. In the middle of opening these presents, there came a knock at the door, and when I opened it, I found our next-door neighbor Mary Holcomb standing on our stoop, holding out a little gift-wrapped box in her hand. The Holcombs were a wonderful elderly couple. They had a son who had served in World War II as a gunner on an Avenger, a torpedo bomber, the same kind George H. W. Bush flew during the war, and their son's plane had been shot down. No one survived. Everyone inside got really quiet when they saw Mrs. Holcomb, because she had this

My parents and me.

incredibly serious look in her eye. She handed me the box and said, "Johnny, this gift is for your mother, but you have to carry it." I was stunned and didn't know what to say. "It's my hope that it will protect you and your mother from what I've had to go through all these years."

When I opened it, I found a beautiful sterling silver Saint Christopher medal inside. Saint Christopher was the patron saint of travelers, and the medal depicted a Christ child on Christopher's shoulder. It was beautifully done. At first I didn't understand what Mary had meant, but then I realized that she had prayed for me to return home alive, and the medal had been blessed with her prayers, which she believed would protect me while I was in Vietnam. As soon as my father saw the medal, he said, "Come on, let's go out in the garage, and we'll put a hole in it and then you can put it on your dog tags." We knew this was important shit. So we went straight into the garage, where Dad zipped a hole in the medal and I strung it onto my dog tags. I came right back inside and showed Mrs. Holcomb. She seemed pleased and moved to see me wearing it, and I knew right then that although I had been raised Methodist, not Catholic, if I was going to make it back alive, I could never lose sight of my Saint Christopher medal.

On my last night home, I had a hard time saying goodbye to my folks and Karen. For the first time in my life I was in love, and I was planning on marrying Karen and spending the rest of my life with her. I wanted to have the ceremony as soon as I got home. But she wanted to go to college and was in line to get a full athletic scholarship, because she was a real tomboy who had set all kinds of state records in swimming. She had her mind set on marrying after college, but I planned to go on a full offensive as soon as I was back, to try to accelerate the schedule. At least that's what I was thinking when I left. As I packed my seabag, with my parents sitting there quietly in my room watching me, I began wondering if I'd ever see my home again. I knew there was a very good chance that I wouldn't, and the thought of not returning weighed heavily upon me for the first time.

A large group of family members and friends accompanied me to the airport, including my mom, dad, grandma, uncle and aunt, Karen, and Karen's mother. I had a hell of a crowd there with me to say goodbye. We all knew where I was going and that this could be the last time we would all be together. My father had tears in his eyes, and it was one of the few times I had ever seen him cry. Years later, he told me that as he watched me walk out of the terminal across the field and to the airplane, he was convinced he'd never see me again.

CHAPTER 5

Shipping Out

A FTER RETURNING to Camp Pendleton, I entered the staging battalion, in which we spent four weeks getting ready to deploy. The first two weeks were on the main side of the base, where we took care of administrative tasks, such as writing our wills and getting our equipment squared away. Every Marine was issued two seabags. In one, you neatly folded and packed all of the stuff that you wouldn't need in Vietnam, all your winter gear. In the other, you packed up your gear for the tropics. Then all of us had to scramble to write a letter home that would accompany a package of stuff we wouldn't be taking to Vietnam, asking them to hold on to it so we wouldn't have to replace it all later. We went through this final phase of training, excited and apprehensive for what lay ahead, all the while making another group of close friends, a wonderful circle of guys with whom we would deploy to Vietnam.

Billy Petrossi and I were having a great time one day, until it came time for our battalion inspection. When the battalion commander entered the barracks, we all ran beside our racks and stood at attention. He came through and inspected our "crap on the rack" or "junk on the bunk." In the Marine Corps, everything you own, and two seabags full of gear, if folded properly, should be able to fit on your rack, and there was a specific place for everything. The battalion commander came through quietly, never addressing us directly. Whenever he saw something out of place, he would mutter something in a low voice to the first sergeant, who would then get right up in the Marine's face, screaming things like "You folded those fucking Skivvies wrong, you dumb shit! You're supposed to be able to see your name stamp on those socks!" The Marine Corps was totally unforgiving about the minutiae, because it was the little shit that got you killed.

I was standing there by my rack, sweating bullets, while this lieutenant colonel came through and looked over my gear. Suddenly he swung back around, stopped right in front of me, and looked at me really hard. He said, "What's your name?" And I said, "Sir, Private First Class John Musgrave." And he said, "Where are you from, Private?" "Sir, Missouri, sir," I replied. He asked me my MOS, and I told him 0311, and he just kept bearing down on me, asking these seemingly normal questions, but I knew in my heart that something was wrong and he was just working his way up to it. Finally, he took a long pause, moved even closer, looked me straight in the eye, and said, "How old are you, Marine?" And I said, "Sir, the private is eighteen years old, sir." And then, as if I were lying to him, he said, "What's your birth date?" To which I replied, "Sir, 12 May 1948." And he said, "Get me your ID card." Now, our ID cards had to be displayed in a certain place during the crap on the rack inspection. So I had to break the position of attention to go over, get my ID card, come back, brace again, and present my ID card to him. The commander held my ID card up to my face, to make sure I hadn't given him someone else's ID card. He then turned it over to inspect the date of birth. Upon reading it, he kind of deflated, handed the card back to me with this sober look, and said, "All right, Marine. Good luck," something he didn't say to anyone else in my platoon. A little later, I saw my platoon commander and asked what the exchange had been about, and he said that the battalion commander couldn't believe I was eighteen, and it hit him so hard that he just kept saying, "The kid's too young. He doesn't look eighteen. Are you sure he's eighteen?" As he told me this, it suddenly occurred to me that if he had demanded an investigation into my age, I would have been held back and wouldn't have been able to go to Vietnam with my buddies, a truly sobering thought.

We spent the second two weeks up in the hills of Camp Pendleton doing training exercises, such as day and night patrols, raids, and ambushes. During this final stretch, there were two other instances where I feared I might not be able to go overseas with my friends. The first was the result of a back injury I had sustained during basic training, when I slipped and fell on an obstacle. I didn't notice I was hurt until later that night. When I lay down on my rack, which wasn't exactly a Posturepedic mattress, I found that my lower back was killing me, and for the rest of training it took about thirty minutes before I could finally drift off to sleep each night, no matter how tired I was. It hadn't really improved during training. So I decided to get my back looked at when we were over on the main side of base with the staging battalion. The Navy doctor told me that I had a lower back injury and gave me some medicine that immediately made me sick, and he assigned me light duty for the next few days. Then he gave me a date to return for further examination to determine what course of treatment they were going to take. The day I was supposed to return to the Navy hospital was the day we were scheduled to load onto the ship. So I didn't show up for the appointment, and I could have been court-martialed for it. I was openly disobeying the direct orders of a naval officer, and that whole day I was half expecting them to come and get me, but then I thought to myself that once they found out that I was on the ship, they'd probably leave it be, or maybe they wouldn't even notice I was missing. Either way, I figured it was worth the risk, because they could have taken a second look at my back and quickly determined that I wasn't fit to deploy. Thankfully, I recovered pretty quickly.

Another moment when I thought I might not be able to go overseas with my friends occurred after a series of inspections by NCOs from the Recon Training Battalion. The Recon Marines were the elite division that conducted unconventional special operations behind enemy lines. They came through three times looking for volunteers. A few guys stepped forward, but not in the numbers they wanted. The NCOs would come down the row and judge you by your physical appearance. If you looked like a potential Recon Marine, they would thump you in the chest with a forefinger and ask if you wanted to volunteer. Over those three inspections, I was asked twice if I wanted to volunteer. Although I wasn't a big, stocky guy, it turned out that they weren't looking for just muscle mass. They had their own special formula, which for the life of me I couldn't figure out. But I wasn't about to volunteer. I was hell-bent on going to Vietnam with my buddies.

During the last week, they gave one final inspection. A few other guys volunteered because it meant they got to stay home longer. One of the NCOs came up, punched me in the chest, and asked if I wanted to volunteer. And I said, "No, sir. Not right now. I don't." But he wouldn't take no for an answer and said that they would take down my name and service number and that I was to report to Camp Horno on Thursday. I dug in my heels and insisted, "I'm not interested in going to Recon right now. I'm getting ready to go to Vietnam." And the NCO got up in my face and said, "This isn't about what you want. It's about what the Marine Corps wants. We'll see you at Camp Horno on Thursday," which was the day after the ship was going to sail. I wasn't about to get separated from Billy and Gordy and all of my other buddies. That wasn't going to happen; they'd have to kill me first. So when the day came to ship out, I boarded the ship and sweated bullets until they threw off the lines and we started moving away from the dock. As we did, I breathed a big sigh of relief that neither the hospital staff nor the Recon sergeant had come rushing down to get me. By then, I had equated survival with being with my buddies, so I had done everything I could to ship out with them.

During that final week, I called home one last time. My dad said, "Would you like to come home for your last weekend? Would they let you do that?" And I said, "Sure, Dad," but I was lying through my teeth. "Since you're going to be away next Christmas, we'd like to give you your Christmas present early," he said. And so they bought me a ticket home for my last weekend. When we got our liberty cards that last weekend, we were granted a two-hundred-mile radius of travel, and if you went beyond that limit, you were considered out of bounds. If I got caught outside the radius, technically I would have an unauthorized absence, UA, and I could have been court-martialed and sent to prison for trying to miss a movement. So until I got on that plane home, I was profoundly worried. But as soon as I stepped on that plane, my nerves steadied, and I felt a wave of calm pass over me as my newfound sense of self-confidence took hold. I had a mission and I was going to see it through. When I arrived in Kansas City at about ten o'clock that night, I walked down the airplane ramp, across the field, and into the terminal and saw Mom, Dad, and Karen waiting to greet me. But instead of joy, I was suddenly paralyzed with dread as a Marine Corps major and two military policemen in dress greens walked up beside my parents and fiancée. I felt my heart drop out of my ass and thought, *Oh, God, they caught me, and the girl of my dreams is standing right there. What do I do?*

But I was a Marine and I figured I had no choice but to brass it through. I walked right up to the major, cracked a salute, and said, "Good evening, sir." Until that very moment, I was convinced the major had been looking at me, but it turned out he had been looking over my shoulder at a prisoner who was being brought off an airplane and into his custody. "Good evening, Marine. Have a nice leave," he replied, before walking off. If he had asked me for my travel orders, all I would have been able to show him was a liberty card from Camp Pendleton, which would have raised suspicions, but thankfully he didn't ask and seemed genuinely appreciative that I had saluted and addressed him. Generally, when out in the civilian world, we weren't required to salute officers, but we were required to acknowledge them. My saluting him had been an additional sign of respect.

Mom and Dad had been standing there looking at the major too, wondering why the MPs were at the gate and worried that maybe I had done something wrong, so they were looking a bit stricken when I first saw them. As soon as I moved past the major, Karen squealed as she ran up and threw her arms around me, just as I'd always dreamed she would. We all went out for a late dinner and drove home. Then Dad gave me the keys to his new car, and I drove Karen to her place, which took a couple of hours. The next night, they left us with the house, and Dad said there was a full tank of gas in the car, which would get us to Oklahoma and back, in case we had a mind to go there. You could get married in Oklahoma under the age of twenty-one in those days, and lots of kids did it. My parents had eloped during World War II in Amarillo, Texas, when my father was stationed there in 1943; so his suggestion that we drive to Oklahoma was pointed and clear. We didn't make a break for Oklahoma that night. Karen wasn't ready to elope, and neither was I, but when Dad left me the car that night, I knew that he and Mom endorsed Karen becoming a member of our family, and that meant the world to me.

It was a beautiful weekend, and to make it last, I reserved a seat on the latest flight out of Kansas City to Los Angeles. We all went to the airport again. This time Karen, my parents, my brother, Butch, and his wife, Gloria, came to send me off. I said goodbye to my family in the terminal, but Karen walked out with me onto the runway to bid me farewell. It was a perfect Hollywood moment, young lovers being separated by war. We stood on the tarmac, holding each other, crying, and kissing, as snow cascaded down from the clouds. We'd seen this movie hundreds of times, and now it was happening to us. Karen didn't want to let go, and I didn't either. By this point, all of the passengers had boarded, and a ground patrol came over to tell us they needed me on the plane. But I wasn't moving. Then one of the stewardesses came out of the plane and said, "Sir, we hate to break this up." And I said, "Ma'am, I'm leaving for Vietnam in three days. I'll be there in just a minute." The stewardess apologized and went back inside. The next person who came out was the pilot, and he said, "Excuse me, son, but we've got to take off. It's snowing and they're talking about closing this runway. I'm sorry, but we need to get off the ground." And he apologized to Karen and saluted her, which made us both feel terribly grown up. It took all the strength within me to pull away from her and walk up those stairs. Before ducking into the plane, I turned around one last time, and she was still standing there, sobbing, and I thought my heart was going to break. Then I climbed into the plane, and we took off.

Just about everyone except for the pilot came back to speak to me during the flight, to ask about Karen and when we were going to get married, and if I carried a picture of her with me, and to tell me how sorry they were that we couldn't spend more time together. They were all so incredibly kind that I've never been able to forget it. Leaving that second time made me feel really old, because I was being separated from everything and everyone I loved. I was never more aware of just how much I had to defend. Over the next eleven and a half months in the jungle, I traveled back to that moment over and over again in my mind, because it was one of the most beautiful memories of my life, which my parents had made possible by sending me that ticket home. I wrote them many times to thank them for what they had given me, a gift that none of my close friends got to experience before they left and for which I will always be grateful.

On Wednesday morning, we loaded our seabags on buses waiting to take about a thousand of us down to the docks in San Diego. As we approached the water, we saw the big gray troopship, the USNS *General W. H. Gordon,* a Merchant Marine vessel that evoked the countless documentaries I had seen featuring Marines going off to the Pacific during World War II. Most Marines went to war on passenger jets. So I counted myself lucky that it was my turn to climb aboard a troopship, as so many other Marines had done before us. We expected the conditions on board to be Spartan, at best, with many of us crammed into tight quarters, but it turned out to be pretty comfortable.

A day later, we pulled into San Francisco Bay. We docked there for three days, long enough to load twenty-five hundred Army troops onto the ship. We weren't allowed to leave. We weren't even allowed to go down and stand on the dock. They weren't taking any chances on us, and so they kept us on the ship. The only people who came down to see us were Chinese prostitutes, and they didn't come to work; they just came to talk to the guys. They yelled up to us, things like "When you get back, come and see me!" and of course there were plenty of guys lining the rail and talking back to them. Those were the only civilians who came down to see a few thousand American boys off to fight a war on their behalf. The Chinese girls came back the day we were shipping out, and an Army band set up on the dock and started playing music. They waved at us and wished us luck, while the band played "The Star-Spangled Banner," the Army anthem, and the Marine Corps Hymn. The enormity of the moment and the voyage ahead really started to hit home. Once the ship shoved off, it wasn't going to dock again until Okinawa, and we wouldn't be allowed off then, either. It was our last moment in the United States.

As the ship pulled out into San Francisco Bay, everyone was up on the deck and we were all really excited to finally be shipping out. As we passed close to Alcatraz, that infamous prison, a few guys joked about how they'd rather spend the next year

*Me and Pat Van Buren, right. Just after this picture was taken,
we went ashore at Vietnam.*

there than where we were headed. It was late afternoon, and the
harbor was littered with cruise boats packed full of tourists who
were taking in the sights. A couple of the boats came up close
enough for us to hear the tour guides over their PA systems,
saying, "Ladies and gentlemen, that ship over there off to your
right is carrying a shipload of young Soldiers and Marines who
are going to Vietnam to fight for our country. How about giving
them a cheer?" The tourists all cheered.

Some of the guys had what we called "dry pack" prophylac-
tics, unlubricated condoms, which they got from the corpsmen
whenever they went on liberty, and they started blowing them
up into balloons, tying them off, and throwing them over for
the civilians. I don't think the civilians had any idea what they
were, but it was all in good fun. And it was thrilling to be an

eighteen-year-old kid from Sugar Creek, Missouri, on a troopship crossing the ocean toward the other side of the world.
As we passed under the Golden Gate Bridge, a huge group of
us crowded as close as we could to the fantail and just stood
there looking at the bridge and the coastline. You could have
heard a flea fart. I kept staring off at the horizon, unable to
tear myself away. *This look has got to last me,* I thought. I also
knew that it might be the last time I saw my homeland. It was
an intense moment. We stood there stone silent as the main-
land disappeared from view. Then Billy turned around without
saying a word, grabbed the hand of the guy next to him, and
shook it. And before I knew it, all of my close buddies were
solemnly shaking each other's hands. Then other guys, a little
farther down, saw us doing it, and they started shaking hands,
too. Pretty soon everyone on the ship was shaking hands, this
big group of kids, most of whom did not know each other. And
nobody said a fucking word.

BOOK TWO

THE KILL ZONE

CHAPTER 6

First Contact

THE NIGHT BEFORE WE ARRIVED in Vietnam, Billy and I snuck out on the deck. We knew it would probably be the last time we could speak privately, and as we gazed out at the sea, I took the opportunity to tell him about this bad feeling I had in my gut that I wasn't going to make it home. He listened to my premonition and then asked, "Are you sure you're not just imagining this?" And I said, "I ain't imagining it, Billy. I just have the feeling that this isn't going to work out for me the way I had hoped."

We changed the subject and talked about Billy's girlfriend, Dawn, for a while and about Karen. Then Billy looked at me and said, "Man, I'll be so sad if something happens to you. You can't die. We've got plans." And I said, "I know. I won't, if I've got anything to say about it. I've just got this feeling. Never had it before." Billy grinned, slapped me on the shoulder, and said, "Well, Musky, I don't want you to worry about me, because I know I'm going to make it." Billy was a very devout Catholic, and this gave him remarkable clarity and confidence. "God has a plan for my life," he said. I believed in God, too, but I wasn't so sure about what His plans were for me. "Billy," I said, "I can't tell you how good it makes me feel to know that you're sure." Billy smiled and said, "I just wish I could somehow share it with you." *Me, too,* I thought. Billy was one of those guys who could do anything. I was never really worried about whether he would make it. If any of us would, it would be Billy. Unfortunately, I was wrong. About ten months later, Billy went out to rescue a badly wounded Marine in Quang Nam Province and was shot in the chest. He died a couple of days later, leaving his young wife, Dawn, a widow. They had experienced only five days of wedded bliss on R&R before he returned to the bush and was subsequently killed in action. But that night on the deck, I was the one with a horrible sense of foreboding about what awaited me in Vietnam.

The next morning, we were issued our orders and given our embarkation numbers. Amphibious landing crafts started pulling up next to the ship, loading up with Marines, and taking them to Da Nang Harbor, a former French colonial port in the middle of Vietnam on the coast of the South China Sea. When I got my orders, I couldn't believe my eyes. All my friends' orders read First or Third Marine Division, and their duty assignments were infantry. Mine, however, read, "First Marine Division, First Military Police Battalion." *What the fuck is this?* I thought. *I'm not a military policeman. I'm a rifleman.* I ran over to my NCO in a panic and said, "Gunny, what's this all about? I don't understand this. I'm infantry." And he said, "I don't know. This is the Marine Corps, son. Remember, it's not always about what you want. It's about what the commandant wants." I was shaken and confused. All of my buddies were going to be infantry, and it looked as if I were going to have a puss job. I didn't enlist in the Marine Corps to become a policeman. I signed up to fight on the front lines. Of course, they were all congratulating me. Billy even came over and said, "See. It's going to be okay. I'll see you in thirteen months."

As I said final goodbyes to my friends, knowing that we would soon be separated and scattered across Vietnam, there was rock music playing in the background. It must have been Armed Forces Radio coming out of Da Nang, and it was a song by Buffalo Springfield that I had never heard before. "There's something happening here," the lyrics went. And I remember being struck by the line "There's a man with a gun over there, telling me I've got to beware." Pat, Billy, Gordy, and I looked at each other, and I thought, *Uh-oh. I hope that ain't an omen.* I turned to them, "You all write to me when you get to your unit so I'll know what company you're in, and I'll try to get up to you as soon as I can."

Then it was my turn to load onto a landing boat. I didn't have a rifle, just a seabag slung over my back, and in my mind I couldn't stop replaying all of those beach landings I'd seen in World War II documentaries. Images of lagoons filled with hundreds of dead Marines who never even touched the beach flooded the backs of my eyelids. I couldn't help but think of Iwo Jima, where countless Marines were blasted right off the sand in the bloodiest battle in Marine Corps history. Of course, we knew that there wouldn't be anyone shooting at us as we pulled into Da Nang Harbor in South Vietnam, far from where our troops were fighting the Vietcong, but I still sort of expected to be fired on the moment the ramp dropped. I was a combat Marine coming off a troopship, making an amphibious landing, and I was pretty pumped. It was a bit of a letdown to be met on the beach by a bunch of kids selling Coca-Colas and fuck books.

Every set of orders included a number that corresponded to a truck. So for a few minutes, we walked the beach searching for trucks that bore our numbers. I approached what seemed to be the right one, and the driver said, "Let me see your orders. First MPs. Yup, this is the right truck. Climb on board." We loaded into the back of the open truck, and of course we'd heard stories back home about how wire mesh had to be placed over the windows of buses so people wouldn't be able to toss grenades into them, and I couldn't help wondering if we were sitting ducks in the back of the truck. All of us were nervous, and we had a long drive ahead to a Seabee camp where Bravo Company was quartered.

As we began driving through Da Nang, the first thing that hit me was the overwhelming odor. It smelled like human waste, rotting food, decay, and foliage so new, thick, and exotic it felt as if you could grab ahold of the leaves and pull them into you. I'd been to Tijuana once, which was my only point of reference for an undeveloped country, but I'd never smelled anything like Vietnam. I'd also never seen women going to the bathroom on the side of the road in broad daylight, or prostitutes openly walking the streets. As we passed through the city, we saw all of these "dog patches," or rows of whorehouses, and the girls were waving to us and trying to get the drivers to stop the trucks, but we kept rolling right through. We were all wide-eyed at so many of the sights. Back home, we'd been told that the Vietcong wore black pajamas, but just about everyone we saw was dressed in what looked like black pajamas. For a few moments, I think we all believed they'd made a mistake and put us in the wrong end of Vietnam. "Jesus Christ," some genius blurted out.

"This place is full of fucking foreigners!" It only took a couple of seconds for me to realize that I was the genius who came up with that observation. I was horrified and embarrassed, but it had just slipped out, right in front of God, the guys, and everybody else. There was no taking it back. And it was a pretty good indication of just how naive and nervous I was at the time.

What I didn't understand when I received my orders, but soon learned, was that I had been assigned to an infantry platoon attached to a military police battalion. Each battalion was made up of four companies, only one of which, Charlie Company, was composed of actual military policemen. I was in Bravo Company in a reinforced rifle platoon, which was the combat reaction force for Da Nang East Compound. So if anybody attacked us, we were the first to go out and fight the fire. And that's pretty much what we did. We ran day and night patrols, day and night ambushes, and blocking forces for operations, if they needed roadblocks. We'd put on MP helmets for the roadblocks so the trucks would stop for us. If we didn't wear MP helmets, the trucks wouldn't even slow down, figuring we were just a bunch of grunts looking for a ride. We also had to project the authority of law enforcement to the Vietnamese, because they were mainly the people we were stopping at checkpoints—in trucks, taxis, school buses, and jeeps. If civilians saw the MP helmets, they wouldn't be as afraid as when a bunch of grunts were stopping them. They were wary of the grunts and went out of their way to avoid them, probably for good reason.

We arrived at Camp Adenir about an hour after leaving the ship. Camp Adenir was located across the river and down the road, south toward Marble Mountain and Marine Air Group 16. Before we got to Marble Mountain we passed the Naval Hospital, where hundreds of Marines' lives were saved. A couple of the other guys and I jumped off the truck with our seabags slung over our shoulders and reported to the duty hut, where we got our orders. We were issued our M14s, flak jackets, helmets, canteens, and bayonets, and we each drew a couple of bandoliers of ammunition—as many magazines as we wanted to carry to the fort—and three hand grenades. We slept in tents on wooden platforms with screens and roofs made of aluminum. At the time, they seemed pretty luxurious, and I'd certainly slept in worse conditions at Camp Pendleton. We each got issued a cot and a footlocker, and I went in and started unloading my seabag. We were told to make up our racks and relax, and we didn't pull duty that day, because they knew we were exhausted from the trip and wanted to give us some time to get our "land legs."

As the day wore on, I started meeting the guys I was going to be serving with, which at first was awkward, because everybody was new and a bit tentative. It was always a nervous time when you were the new guy and you didn't know whom to try to befriend and whom to avoid. Usually, the first guy you met, the one who was friendliest, was the guy nobody liked, and he was just trying to make a new friend. And as it turned out, the first guy I met was that guy. He ended up helping me a lot and managed to score some gear for me from the Seabees, the Naval Construction Battalions, which made my area a little more livable. He wasn't very intelligent, which wasn't a big deal, but he turned out to be a raving racist, which made it hard to be his friend. I was always grateful to him for the way he welcomed me, and I never gave him the cold shoulder, but I told him that his prejudice and bigotry weren't for me, and we didn't hang out together for very long.

My squad leader, who led three fire teams, each composed of four men, was a huge cowboy from Montana. An infantry squad leader is a noncommissioned officer, or NCO, who carries out the orders of the platoon commander and is responsible for the discipline, conduct, and well-being of the men in his squad, as well as the maintenance of their weapons and equipment. If you wanted a picture postcard of the perfect Marine, that would have been him. He could have done anything in the Corps. To my great disbelief, though, he had been drafted. He was the first draftee I met over there. I just couldn't believe it. He was an outstanding Marine and a wonderful squad leader, but he was also happy to tell everybody he met about how they had to shanghai his ass into the Marine Corps.

My fire team leader—each fire team includes a team leader/grenadier, an automatic rifleman, an assistant automatic rifleman, and a rifleman—had already been in the country ten months, and he was also really good. Our sergeant, Jerry Lineberry, had a Force Recon MOS. Force Recon were an elite group of Marines trained to conduct independent special operations from behind enemy lines. He was Airborne and Scuba Qualified and looked just like the Charles Atlas ads—six feet four, super squared away, always ramrod straight. He also had an incredible sense of humor and, when he heard me say my name was Musgrave, nicknamed me Mushroom right off the bat, which I loved. The day we met, I took the risk of cracking a joke and was thrilled to make him laugh. It was always a risk to be the new guy making a crack in front of an E-5, but he thought I was funny. He slapped me hard on the back and said, "You're going to be okay, Mushroom." I always felt good when Sergeant Lineberry was with us. He was an aggressive patroller and even more aggressive on combat reaction calls. If something was coming down and Sergeant Lineberry volunteered to move out, I'd always jump to be selected to go with him, because when I looked at him, I thought, *That's what I want to be like when I'm an E-5.* He liked to carry a grease gun, an M3 .45-caliber subma-chine gun from World War II. I tried carrying one on a couple of patrols, when I was walking point and had my choice. I thought it made me look like Steve McQueen in *Hell Is for Heroes,* but as I soon learned walking point, you can't hit shit with it. You would almost have to stand on the enemy's shoulders and stick the barrel into his mouth to hit him. What I didn't fully under-stand at the time was how mismatched Sergeant Lineberry was with us, a Force Recon Marine in the police battalion. Years later, I learned that he had been pulling out what little hair he had left every day, ranting and raving about how he couldn't go out to join the real action.

One of the first things they had us do in the police battalion was run roadblocks. We had to stop traffic and get all of the Vietnamese who came our way out of their trucks and jeeps. Then we'd search their vehicles and belongings for contraband. On any given day, we'd find bullets and hand grenades, military equipment and stolen typewriters, and we had to confiscate all of it. Having these eyeball-to-eyeball interactions with the Vietnamese was a good experience in the long run, even though it made me uneasy, because they all looked like the enemy to me, especially those who had traveled to the city from the bush. We had to man those roadblocks twenty-four hours a day. We often ended up stopping vehicles at night, which was pretty dangerous, or we pulled day shifts, which were mostly just tedious.

Three days in, I pulled my first night patrol, and I was ner-vous as hell, having heard that night patrols were among the most terrifying missions in the war, so they put me in the cen-ter of the squad. It was a moonlit night, so I had some visibil-ity. Most night patrols were like sticking your head up a black

*This is the way I dressed for patrols (I always wore my flak jacket and rifle).
I was down south when this was taken.*

cat's ass. You couldn't see anything. But that first time out, I could see fairly well, and whenever the point held up his left fist or dropped down, to signal danger, I had no trouble tracking it. In boot camp, we trained for night patrols by learning "to pass the word." The Drill Instructor would whisper something to the first guy in the column, and then he had to whisper it down the line. By the time it got to the last guy, it didn't in any way resemble what had been said up front. So we learned the importance of passing the word. Over time, we got pretty good at it.

That night on my first patrol, when I saw the guy in front of me squat and then scoot out a bit, my ears trained in on him and I heard him whisper, "Check, points, check." We took our positions so he could watch the guy in front of him, and I waited and waited for him to say something or signal back to me. I was staring at him intently—locked on—but he wasn't moving. So, eventually, I went, "*Pssst. Psssst.*" But he did not answer my "*pssst.*" So I scooted ahead a bit and stood in a bush. At this point, not only was I lost, but all the guys behind me were lost because of me, and I started to panic. Then I remembered what I had been taught in boot camp, that panic kills more Marines than bullets, and I decided to just squat down where I was and didn't move. I was the new guy and was convinced that I had just proven myself to be one dumb motherfucker. Five humiliating minutes passed before they came back and found me. The whole time I was thinking, *Boy, are they going to chew me up now.* But they didn't say a word. We just went on with the patrol as if nothing happened.

It would be my first night under fire, and I did not react well. When we started to take fire, I discovered that incoming tracers, when aimed directly at me, are a hell of a lot scarier than outgoing tracers. No amount of training can really prepare you for it. Of course, downrange, when the rounds are coming at you, it's a whole different ball game, but that first night on patrol I kept thinking, *Why is he shooting at me? I've never done anything to him.* I felt more like a terrified child on a playground than an automatic rifleman upon whom the squad was depending. The rounds were coming in, and for some reason I bypassed the selector switch on my rifle, which adjusts the weapon to automatic mode. I was supposed to be putting bullets downrange with my automatic rifle, but—while the rest of the guys fired more shots—I had frozen up and wasn't doing my job. The squad leader yelled at me to shoot, and I pretended I couldn't hear him because I was paralyzed with fear. He came over and kicked me hard and screamed, "Fire your weapon!" At this point, I was more afraid of him than of the guy who was shooting at me. Suddenly my hands sprang into action, and I started firing downrange. The whole thing lasted only a few seconds. Nobody got hit, but to me it had been the Battle of Gettysburg in Vietnam. It had embarrassed me even more than it scared me.

On the way back in from patrol, I was one sad puppy. I knew I was going to get ripped by these guys when we debriefed after patrol. When it came time to talk about what happened, all that the squad leader said was, "We got separated. The chain broke with you." And I said, "Yeah, I thought I was looking right at him, but it turned out to be a bush." To which he said, "You did a great job." And I thought, *Wait a minute. It's coming. He's going to call you a dumb shit.* But instead, he said, "You did the right thing. You stayed stock-still. You didn't move. This happens to everybody, and when it does, don't move. If you move, you won't be where we expect you to be, or we'll end up bumping into each other or shooting each other. You were right to stay where you were." Then my squad leader looked me up and down. He asked if I was okay and said, "I kicked you awful hard." I told him I was okay and that I needed the kick and expressed how sorry I was about what happened. "Don't worry about it," he said, "this is scary shit. Now you know what it's like and you got it out of your system. Just don't do it again. You're an automatic rifleman for a reason, and we need you out there."

The rest of the guys teased me, which was fine, and a few of them came up and said, "Man, I did worse than that the first time." It was a good feeling to be with this group of guys and know I could fuck up. If I had fucked up like that in training, I would have been thrashed by the Drill Instructors and people would have given me unlimited amounts of horseshit, but these guys were professionals. They told me to focus on what I did right and next time do both things right. And I did.

One night, we got called out as the combat reaction force for Da Nang East Compound at nine or ten o'clock. The sirens started blaring, and we sprang into action. It was just like being a fireman. We grabbed our gear, threw it on, ran out to the six-by truck, jumped on board, and—as soon as we cleared the gate—locked and loaded. We could be called out at any moment, day or night, but generally it was at night, because we were in a heavily populated area. That night, as we jumped into the truck, Marines were throwing cases of hand grenades in the back, and I thought, *Damn. We've never done that before.* There was a big prisoner of war camp up the road, and the POWs were rioting, so we were being sent up there to back up the staff, because the last thing they wanted was a few thousand VC prisoners of war running around Da Nang.

As we pulled up to the compound gate, Sergeant Lineberry jumped out of the truck, got a debrief, came back, and said, "Okay, this is what's going down. They're taking control of the compound." Pointing at six Marines, he said, "I want you to go and back up a group of Marines over there." Then he asked for four volunteers to go with him, and as always I raised my hand and followed his lead. "All right," he said. "Now let me tell you what we're going to do. We're going to drive this truck right through the gate." He had us break open the cases of hand grenades. Each one came in a little cardboard container. You had to pull the tape off, then pull the hand grenade out and straighten the cotter pins before it was ready to go. He had us empty the crates and get the frags ready. We put four sandbags in each corner of the back of the six-by, we each grabbed a bag of frags, and we switched the selectors to rock and roll our M14s on.

"We're going to go straight through that gate, and we're going to drive right into the crowd, and we're going to throw these hand grenades for all they're worth while laying down full automatic fire, and we're going to kill every motherfucker we can. And maybe we can break this thing, and the rest of the guys will give up," Sergeant Lineberry said. My father always told me never to volunteer on a mission, but Sergeant Lineberry was pumped up, and so I was pumped, too, but I also had a sinking feeling that something could go terribly wrong. There were five of us in the truck, plus the driver and his bodyguard riding shotgun, which hardly seemed like enough Marines to stop a riot, given that the compound was jammed with a couple thousand enemy grunts and combat vets. But I had such confidence in Sergeant Lineberry that I knew they couldn't kill him, and if they couldn't kill him, they couldn't kill me.

We fired up the truck, rolled around, and Sergeant Lineberry yelled out, "Open that gate!" while ordering all the other guys that were lined up around the fence to lay down suppressive fire for us. If we ran out of hand grenades and ammunition, he said, we'd come back, resupply, and go back in. Well, as fate would have it, just before we hit the gate, a bunch of officers arrived at the compound, delayed the order, and held us back. We never went in. The riot just petered out. To this day, I'm not sure what happened. The POWs took over the compound and trashed a bunch of stuff, and then I guess they figured they were getting three square meals a day and sleeping on cots and that it wasn't so bad, after all. They made their point, and we didn't have to bust through that gate, M14s and hand grenades blazing. But our readiness to do so was a sign of our unwavering confidence in Sergeant Lineberry.

Decades later, a friend of mine told me he was going to visit the Wall—the Vietnam Veterans Memorial in Washington, D.C.—and asked if there was anybody I wanted him to look up. I gave him twenty names and then went back to look at the directory to make sure I had gotten the spelling right, when, for some reason, I opened to the Ls and stumbled upon the name Jerry Lineberry. It turned out that he was killed during his second tour, which came as a shock, because Sergeant Lineberry planned to keep going back to Vietnam until there wasn't a war to go back to. He also earned the Navy Cross, the second-highest decoration for valor in combat, which did not come as a surprise. I immediately looked up the description of his Navy Cross commendation in another book, and it described him rallying troops after all the officers in his unit had been killed, distributing ammo, and fearlessly leading. I broke down and started sobbing. My buddy on the phone said, "Goddamn, what's the matter?" I just couldn't find the words to explain why I could not believe Sergeant Lineberry had been killed. He was the best Marine I knew. We weren't exactly drinking buddies, he was an E-5, or sergeant, and I was a PFC, or private first class, but he always showed affection for me and was eager to teach me things, probably because I still looked as if I were twelve or fifteen years old and reminded him of a younger brother. I still don't understand how he died and I survived. It just doesn't make any sense.

The thing about combat callouts with the First Military Police Battalion was that we never knew what we were going to get. Sometimes we would jump out of the trucks, line up, and be told that some sappers were last seen running through a field. Our job was to go out there, find them, and kill them. And sometimes—most of the time—it turned into a long, boring walk at night, on which we'd be eaten alive by mosquitoes. I loved doing patrols, especially day patrols, because I could see what was going on, and it was the work I had signed up to do, grunt work, carrying a loaded rifle around and facing danger. Night patrols could be arduous and complicated, because we had to pass through a series of checkpoints, where we would call in and tell them our position and our route of movement, including which checkpoint we'd be going to next and in what direction. We would only call back when something came up and we needed to ask for help or instructions. In the beginning on night patrols, to prevent us from accidentally starting a firefight, we were told not to even chamber a round until we were ordered to do so. We had more restrictions than freedom in those days and could not initiate a firefight unless someone was caught in the act or fired on us first and it was almost certain we could drop him. Most of the time, it felt as if our hands were tied, and I really didn't like that feeling.

There were a lot of times in Vietnam when we were taking fire or we were getting ambushed and I never saw anybody. I was shooting at sounds. Our enemies were so well bunkered that you just couldn't see them or reach them, especially with those damn popguns. M16 bullets were so fast and light that they couldn't penetrate the heavy bush. That's why when you had enemy bodies anywhere, everyone was so damn curious about them, because we'd finally be seeing them. Guys would take out their frustrations on them, getting up in their dead faces and saying things like, "Oh, you ain't so fucking bad now, are you, asshole?" and "Made a believer out of you." A believer was a dead enemy Soldier. If he was dead, he believed you were the baddest motherfucker in the valley. That's when you made a believer out of him. You killed him, and it made him believe you were badder than he was.

Inevitably, you reached a point when there was no more emotional involvement in the act of killing than stepping on a bug. You might feel fear or hatred, but those would be the only feelings that could break through. For some guys, it seemed that none of it ever bothered them, and I admired them for it. I wished I could be like them. And I think the reason that the first guy I killed bothered me so much was that we were very close together. If he had been ten meters away when I shot him, it might have been better for me. Then I would have been a little more in control of my fear. But as it stood, when I saw him, only a few feet away, I just stared at him, really taking him in. I didn't know not to then. And he felt it. He turned his head and looked right at me, right in the fucking eye. I have no idea what he could see. Even though I was down, hiding in the foliage, it felt as if I had been set in the middle of a big open field and I was the only thing to see. I had the selector switch on my M14 on full automatic. So right when he looked, the rifle went off. That's the way I describe it, because I did not make a conscious decision to squeeze the trigger. If my training hadn't taken over, he very likely would have killed me, because I would have just sat there and waited to see what he was going to do.

When I shot him, I experienced an immediate sensory overload. My brain could not process all of the information it was receiving. Prior to my first kill, there had been two other big firsts in my life. The first time I kissed a girl, at the Sugar Creek swimming pool. When we finished kissing, I wasn't sure if it had happened. So I thought, *Great, go for another one. Let's see if it really happened.* And the next big one was my first jump out of a plane. I didn't remember the exit at all, no memory whatsoever. One second I was in the door; the next I was under the canopy thinking, *Holy shit, what just happened?*

It was the same with my first kill. Next thing I knew, I was up and standing over him, but I don't remember getting up. I could hear a voice coming out of my throat, which didn't seem as if it were mine, screaming and terrified, "If you move, I'll kill ya!" And the guy was trying to breathe through the holes I had blown through his chest. He would take in a breath, and then it would blow out of those holes in a bloody froth, almost pink. This was accompanied by a horrible gurgling sound. I've never been able to get it out of my head. He was trying hard to cling to life, struggling to breathe, and then I watched the light go out in his eyes. And it struck me that I was the last thing on this earth that that guy saw before he died.

They weren't gooks to me yet. I hadn't yet learned to dehumanize the enemy. This was a guy. I thought about if his mom and dad could see me standing over his dead body, or maybe his grandparents, what would they think of me? I'd been fantasizing about killing people since I was a little kid. All of my heroes killed people. *I was a Marine infantry rifleman,* I thought, *and I was going to kill people. I was going to be a real man.* Only there I was, and I had done it, and the reality was nothing like the fantasy. Killing didn't bother Errol Flynn or John Wayne or Steve McQueen, my cowboy heroes. I thought it was going to be cool. I thought I was going to feel great. Right then, as I stood over that man's body, a flood of thoughts came rushing into my head: *I could go to prison for this. I might go to hell for it. What the fuck am I supposed to do now? I can't tell Mom and Dad about this.* Something wasn't right. I was supposed to feel good. I'd always known this moment was coming. I'd looked forward to it. Now that it was finally here, I wanted to go home. I wasn't a big bad Marine. I was a teenage kid who just wanted his mother to tell him, "It's going to be okay. Don't worry. You'll never have to do this again." But I knew that would never happen. This was the life I had dreamed of. This was the life I had pursued. If only he could have been farther away. It's strange how different things feel up close, when you have proximity to human suffering.

Later, after I had hardened and my hatred had matured and become pure, I would look forward to killing. If you are in the infantry, the road home is paved with the bodies of your dead enemies, and you ain't getting home without them. It's a filthy line of work that is particularly tough on kids.

There is another thing about the killing. It's a lot easier to do when you're terrified. And it gets easier when you learn what is at stake, that every time you squeeze the trigger you may be saving the life of another grunt. Every dead NVA or VC is one less NVA or VC to be killing Marines, and that was consoling. If you somehow lost the fear, it would feel like another day at the office, but I could never lose that fear. I was always scared, but that kept my hatred pure. Sometimes I wonder if any of us would have volunteered if they had put the real experience of killing in our comic books.

One of the other challenges of patrols, even during the daytime, was the possibility of killing civilians, which made me very uneasy, at least at first, and was always a risk around Da Nang, because the place was crawling with civilians. They were everywhere—in the town, on the roads, and in the fields. At times, we would cross the river into some pretty wide-open spaces, but we seldom went anywhere that we didn't see Vietnamese civilians. They had freedom to move around the area, and it could get pretty uncomfortable when we encountered men who were of military age. Of course they weren't in uniform or wearing signs, and so we simply couldn't tell friend from foe. Sometimes I'd look at a guy who gave me bad vibes and think, *I know that son of a bitch is dirty*. But I couldn't do anything about it. This got harder to navigate the longer I was in Vietnam, especially after I saw my first Marine die.

We were out looking for mines and booby traps one day when a Marine up ahead of me stepped on a Bouncing Betty mine. These were pressure-release devices. They didn't detonate when someone stepped on them, but as soon as he stepped off, a mine that looked like a tall can of tomato sauce, packed with hundreds of ball bearings, blew out of the ground—about waist high—and exploded, sending shrapnel in all directions. Usually, the poor guy who stepped on one of these would lose his legs, the guy in front of him would catch a load of ball bearings in his ass and lower spine, and the guy behind him would get hit in his groin and lower abdomen. This was the main reason there was always a wide separation between guys on patrols. The Bouncing Betty was a horrible weapon. It didn't just blow your legs off; it ripped them off, tearing straight through flesh and bones.

This kid was nineteen years old. I didn't know him. He wasn't in our company. He had a daughter back home whom he hadn't met. There were two corpsmen, or Navy medics, working on him when I ran up with battle dressings. His eyes were completely red—no whites at all—I guess from the concussive force of the explosion, which had burst all the blood vessels in his face. He was in shock and kept saying over and over, "What's going to happen to my little girl? Oh, God! What's going to happen to my family?" They gave him a blood transfusion on the field and loaded him onto a helicopter, but he died on the bird, didn't even make it to the Navy hospital, and I was pretty shaken up by it.

Before coming to Vietnam, I had seen lots of people kill or get killed on the silver screen, but after arriving, I soon learned that the reality of killing and witnessing death was a whole lot different from the fantasy. When I killed a man for the first time in combat, I didn't feel cool. I felt sick. All of my buddies were happy for me. They slapped me on the back and said, "He busted his cherry!" extending the metaphor of losing one's virginity to one's first kill. While they were busy congratulating me, I just kept imagining that other guy. *Did he have a daughter or a family? Who or what had he left behind?* But then I also got to thinking, *I'm going to be here a long time, and I don't know how I'm going to make it and stay sane if I have to keep doing this.* I was a human being, and human beings aren't supposed to kill other human beings.

When I saw that kid step on the Bouncing Betty, I had my first major epiphany in Vietnam. In order to adapt and survive, I would have to make a deal with the devil and learn to dehumanize my so-called enemy. I knew it was wrong, but—at the time—it felt like a necessary evil. I didn't have a choice if I wanted to go home. *From this moment forward,* I said to myself, *I will never kill another human being as long as I am in Vietnam. But I will "waste as many gooks" as I can find. I'll "wax as many dinks," "smoke as many zips," "whack as many pigs."* I had seen this racist strategy modeled by my peers, my instructors, my mentors, and my friends, denying the basic humanity of others so those others could be shot, stomped, burned, blown up. But not murdered or killed, because you can't kill a thing. It took me decades to understand that in denying the humanity of the people we were fighting, I was also denying my own humanity, which is the wound that never heals. I might have lived to speak and write about it, but when I made my deal with the devil, a part of me died in Vietnam. And when I saw that first Marine die, I embraced the very attitude I had come to despise in other

Marines. I did it for my own psychological and emotional salvation, and it served me well while I was there, but it has haunted me ever since. In Vietnam, I never again felt any hesitation or harbored any bad thoughts about killing people, and since coming home, I haven't been able to go to sleep at night without being visited by the humans I killed, as well as their families. I discovered after I got home that the dead sleep on your chest.

In war, there's actually a grotesque truth to saying that somebody got wasted. It's the most appropriate thing to say. The patrol would come in from the field, and I would be looking for my buddy, and someone would say, "He got wasted." And I would think to myself, *Yeah, he got wasted all right.* In 1967, the United States was wasting countless American lives in Vietnam. When I think about my time in the bush, I think about all of the lives that were wasted, on all sides, the lives of my buddies, the lives of the formidable men we fought, and the lives of Vietnamese civilians. Looking back now, I feel especially sorry for the Vietnamese civilians. If they tried to help us, they would be killed by the Vietcong or the North Vietnamese Army. And if we found out they had helped the enemy, we would burn down their houses and sometimes even kill them. In order to do our jobs and cope with the reality of what we knew in our hearts to be wrong, we dehumanized Vietnamese civilians too. When you have children fighting your wars, objectifying so-called enemies turns out to be a very useful tool for staying sane and alive. But the sad calculus of war is that what helps us survive dehumanizes us too.

CHAPTER 7

Joining the Varsity Team

AFTER THAT FIRST CONTACT with the enemy down south around Da Nang, I started to feel pretty glad that I had been assigned to an MP unit, dealing only with Vietcong or VC, who were local guerrilla fighters supported by North Vietnamese, and not out in the real bush up in the north chasing the real bad guys, the North Vietnamese Army, or NVA, a highly trained and formidable army. But during those first few weeks, after I had gained some experience and run a few night patrols, my attitude began to shift. Working with the MPs felt like sticking my foot in the water, when what I really wanted to do was swim and go water-skiing. So I started volunteering to walk point, the most dangerous position on patrols, just to crank up the volume a bit. After a couple of months of supporting the MPs, I began to feel really out of place. *I'm a grunt, goddamn it,* I thought to myself, *and I ought to be out there with the other grunts. Here, I'm just pretending like I'm in the infantry.* I wanted to join the varsity team, but that meant waiting until a levy came up, when volunteers could put in their names to go up north and join divisions in need of Marines, and even then I had to have racked up enough time in country to be high enough on the levy to be selected. Throughout 1967, they started coming through pretty regularly asking for volunteers, because the casualties were ramping up in the north. If they asked for three guys, I planned to be one of those three. And the whole time I was hoping and praying to get a levy for the Third Marine Division, which by then had moved up north and was fighting the NVA, where the real action was. Plus all of my buddies were in the Third Marine Division. My good buddy Pat Van Buren was in Echo 2-9, or the Second Battalion, Ninth Marines, Third Marine Division, and so I decided that's where I wanted to go.

After I'd been in country about two months and the casualties were really starting to pick up, it became possible to volunteer or be chosen to go into the grunts. At the time, they were taking only three guys, and there were already three on the waiting list. So when the letter came down saying that I had volunteered and had been accepted, Sergeant Lineberry made a big deal of it, which, of course, made me feel like a million bucks.

He was thrilled for me and also a bit envious, because he desperately wanted to be out in the real bush, and he spoke proudly about my volunteering in front of the other NCOs and anyone else who would listen. It was validating and it made me feel important. I told them I wanted to go to 2-9. "We can't guarantee where you'll end up," the Marine asking for volunteers said, but encouraged me to ask at the assignment desk at Da Nang airfield.

What I didn't know at the time, but soon learned, was that they knew exactly where I'd end up. They were asking for replacements up north because of the heavy casualties sustained by the 1-9, or the First Battalion, Ninth Marines, Third Marine Division, otherwise known as the Walking Dead. By signing up for the Ninth Marines, I had joined that unit and had zero chance of making it into any other. We would be sent to Con Thien, an eastern Marine combat base situated on top of three small hills, just over five hundred feet tall, two miles south of the DMZ, or the demilitarized zone. Due to its elevation, Con Thien, which means "Hill of Angels" in Vietnamese, offered unrestricted views in every direction, making it one of the most contested mounds of earth in the war. We called it the Bull's-Eye and the Graveyard, because so many of us were killed or injured on and around that three-topped hill. Originally established as a Special Forces camp, it was taken over by Marines in December 1966 in support of the McNamara Line, one of the key operational strategies of Secretary of Defense Robert McNamara from 1966 to 1968 to keep NVA forces from crossing into South Vietnam.

When my friend John Covington and I arrived up north and got assigned to 1-9, I was pretty upset about it, but Cov wasted no time and said, "Hey, this is a good unit. I've heard about these guys. Stick with me." Covington was twenty-two, which seemed so much older at the time. We had both been with the First MPs down south, but neither of us felt we belonged there. Cov was the oldest man in the platoon who wasn't a career Marine, and we called him Pop. He always looked out for me and never led me astray. So when he said to stick with him, I did. All of the companies in 1-9 needed replacements, so we were given the opportunity to choose a company. Cov, who had been a pledge for the Delta Tau Delta fraternity, said, "We'll go to Delta Company. That's going to be lucky for us." And because I didn't have any other friends in 1-9, I said, "Okay," and that's how I ended up in Delta Company. All the guys who went to Bravo Company got killed, so in the end Cov was right about Delta being lucky, because neither of us died.

Our first stop was Dong Ha Combat Base, a helicopter base and logistics area northwest of Quang Tri in what was then the northernmost part of South Vietnam, where we waited for the unit to come back in from the bush so we could join it. As we checked in, I was issued my first M16, which I was pretty excited about, at least at first. To my disappointment, it wasn't a new one and they gave me only four clips—just four magazines. By then, I had been carrying an M14 for a few months, and I knew that I wanted as many magazines as I could get my hands on. Four magazines ain't shit. But they said, "That's all we got." Finally, they gave us one canteen each. I'd been in the field already, and I knew you needed more than one canteen to survive out there. It was clear that they were giving us scraps. They didn't even issue us cleaning gear for our rifles, which were not very clean to begin with, because they were casualty rifles. They told us to go up to Delta Med, the medical battalion that was seeing casualties at Dong Ha, and outside Delta Med receiving we would find a pile of equipment that had been stripped off the dead and the wounded. That's where we were supposed to get our extra magazines, our extra canteens, and our jungle boots, if we needed them.

Up at Delta Med, the helicopters were flying in and out at a dizzying pace, hauling in a lot of wreckage. We walked over to a giant pile filled with bloody uniforms, field equipment, pistol belts, and entrenching tools, and that's where I picked up my extra canteens and my entrenching tool. That's where I started grabbing bandoliers of M16 magazines. We didn't have the Army equipment to carry the magazines, so we used ammunition bandoliers. Each had seven pockets, and each pocket would hold a single magazine. We each grabbed at least two bandoliers, which brought us up to eighteen magazines apiece, including the four magazines we had already been issued. That seemed a good start. Some of the guys grabbed metal canteens, saying the plastic ones made the water "taste funny," but I knew to grab a plastic one. Metal canteens had hard plastic caps on little metal chains, and when you unscrewed one, the hard cap would sometimes drop down and strike the canteen, ringing it like a bell. That noise could get your ass killed out in the bush. This was just one of many survival tips I had picked up on night patrols from Sergeant Lineberry.

I had also learned that you never put your entrenching tool in your haversack, the little canvas bag that Marines were issued to carry around everything they own. It had a flap on the back that was specifically designed for the entrenching tool, but you never hooked your entrenching tool to it, because there would be plenty of occasions when you would hear an order to "drop packs," which meant you left your pack behind. And if it was hooked to your haversack, that meant leaving your entrenching tool behind, and a grunt without an entrenching tool could easily get killed. If you were hit or ambushed and couldn't break out, then you had to dig in and get your ass below ground level, because if you were above it, you were going to get shot. The other reason you always needed your entrenching tool handy was that the fucking rifles they gave us didn't work, and when your rifle jammed, an entrenching tool could save your life when you got overrun by the enemy. So you always hooked it to your belt or to the bottom of your flak jacket. That way, it would be with you at all times.

In boot camp, we learned to be experts with our bayonets, because we couldn't count on our rifles to work. The M16s that we were issued in the Third Marine Division came to us already used, passed down to us from the Army. Secretary of Defense McNamara had forced the Army to start using the M16, a notoriously unreliable weapon. McNamara came from Ford and wanted to standardize the military. The Marine Corps held on as long as it could to its trusted select-fire battle rifle, the M14, but by the spring of 1967 we didn't have a choice anymore, and our unit was the first to start using the M16. The biggest problem with the M16 was that if you didn't keep it clean, it wouldn't work. The mythology of the M16 was that it was a "self-cleaning rifle," but believing that shit was a death sentence. When we finally got cleaning equipment for our rifles, we received only one bore rod, one bore brush, and one chamber brush per squad. Each squad leader would assemble the bore rod and tape it to the fore end of his M16, and we all had to share it.

When you fired an M16, the firing pin struck the primer on the end of the shell casing. The primer exploded, which threw a flash into the powder inside the shell casing, which exploded and expanded into gas and launched the bullet out of the shell casing so fast that it flew straight down a steel barrel, which was a very tight fit for that bullet, and moved forward with such force that it blew out of the barrel, faster than the speed of sound. If the rifle was functioning properly, that bullet would travel in a straight line for more than five hundred meters. But the sheer force of each explosion, each time the rifle was fired, caused the shell casing to swell, and because of this, if it was not cleaned properly and regularly, the weapon would inevitably jam. Marines are taught from boot camp to be fanatical about cleaning their weapons, but the M16 had so many problems it didn't matter.

The M16 was not designed for the bush. It was developed for the Air Force to use as a security weapon, inside the wire, on bases, and for this purpose it was more than excellent. It was never meant to be used in a setting in which it would get dirty or would be fired hundreds of times at once. In such a setting, when it jammed from a stoppage or some other malfunction—which happened all the fucking time—the M16 turned into a six-and-a-half-pound plastic club. Because of the M16's poor design, its most dangerous malfunction occurred when the shell casing didn't extract after firing. The casing would stick in the chamber while the bolt flew back to chamber another round. As the bolt went forward it would strip the next round halfway out of the magazine, where it would jam up against the empty case stuck in the chamber. Most of the times when this happened, you couldn't pull the bolt back, because the bolt got jammed halfway between the magazine and the chamber. And you couldn't break the rifle apart to take out the bolt, because the bolt carrier was located halfway in the buffer unit, in the butt of the rifle, and halfway in the receiver. The case would be stuck in the chamber, the bolt would be stuck, and the magazine would be stuck—three different problems that could each keep the rifle from working. In order to get the rifle to operate properly, you had to move the bolt back to the rear, which meant pounding the magazine out of the rifle, which would then release the cartridge that was jammed between the bolt and the chamber. If you managed to pound out the magazine and then pulled the bolt all the way out, then you would call to your squad leader for that single bore rod, which he would pull off the front of his rifle and throw to you. And you would hope to God that he could see you to throw it to you, because often in the bush after the first shot was fired, you didn't see your buddies again until the fight was over. The vegetation was too thick for you to see a man standing an arm's length away. And so if you got the rod thrown to you and it actually reached you and you didn't get shot when you reached up to grab it, then you'd run it down the bore of your rifle, as if you were Davy Fucking Crockett at the Alamo, to punch out that empty case and start the game over again. Chances are if it malfunctioned once, it was going to malfunction every time you squeezed the trigger. So what you had was a single-shot rifle that you had to beat the shit out of in order to get it to work, while the enemy was carrying an AK-47 or an SKS, far superior weapons that could be run over by a tank and would still shoot. We called these "body-bag malfunctions," because they would get you killed. Thousands of Marines were killed with hundreds of rounds of ammunition on them, but they couldn't use any of it. They were bayoneted or beaten to death or shot point-blank by the enemy because their government took away from them a perfectly good rifle that worked, the M14, and forced them to use one that didn't. I will never forgive this government for forcing that rifle on us. It was a betrayal of the highest order.

Combat is terrifying, and if you're carrying a rifle that you can't count on, it's even more terrifying. And when you find the mutilated bodies of dead Marines that have been killed in a hands-on and personal way, with a torn-down rifle beside them that the enemy wouldn't even bother to pick up, it shakes you to your core. One of the recurring nightmares that I know almost every grunt had over there was the one in which our rifles malfunctioned. Or, if they did shoot in the dream, the bullets didn't hurt the NVA. We were so afraid of our rifles not working that even when they did work in our dreams, they did no damage. All of this is to say that when I finally made it to the varsity team, I lost the rifle that I knew I could count on, and it added a whole new level of fear to the exercise.

When I joined the 1-9, I was feeling pretty hot. I'd experienced combat and had been running day and night patrols. I figured I was a professional who knew what he was doing. When the guys came out of the field and I joined them as a replacement, I was wearing brand-new jungle utilities and jungle boots, because the stuff I arrived in was worn out and ripped and I had been resupplied upon arriving. They all thought I was brand-new in country, or what they called a "boot" Marine. "Nah, guys," I told them, "I've been here for months." And they said, "Great, that's good. Who were you with?" And I said, "Bravo Company, a reinforced rifle platoon," not mentioning the MPs, to which they said, "Oh, fuck. That's great. What did you do?" And I said, "Primarily, I walked point." And these guys all looked at each other, as if to say, "Are you shitting me? You walked point?" "That's right," I said, "I walked point," and I was feeling pretty hot about it. After all, I was a point man and proud of it. *Why shouldn't I be?* I thought. Walking point is just about the bravest thing a Marine can do. Of course, I had no idea what I was saying or how different the world I had just entered would be. Down south with the First Marine Division, we had been exclusively fighting the Vietcong. I didn't have the faintest clue what it meant to be in a firefight with the North Vietnamese Army, or NVA. But the first one I was in cured my ass of thinking I was a hotshot.

The NVA all fired on rock and roll. They had the best assault rifle in the fucking world, the AK-47, but they didn't hit you unless they had enough troops. They knew that the biggest advantage they had over us was numbers. They just had more meat on the field than we did, and they used it to overpower us. Down south, we had artillery, which was a game changer, because all they had were mortars and rockets. But up north, not only did they have artillery, but their artillery was better than ours. Their 152s were Russian or Chinese copies that could fire faster and farther than our 155s and 105s. Their 130s could fire faster and farther, too. We had 60-millimeter mortars, and they had 61s, and we had 81-millimeter mortars, and they had 82s, which meant they could use our ammunition if they took it from us, but we couldn't use theirs. The only thing we had over the NVA was airpower. We could "call in God" from the fucking heavens. That's what we called it. But they adapted to our airpower with a simple strategy. The NVA would almost always wait to make contact until the Americans were so close that they couldn't call in air support without calling it on themselves. Their slogan was "When you fight the Americans, hang on to their belts." There were times when we had a choice between getting overrun and killed or, even worse, captured, which meant being tortured and mutilated, and calling in an airstrike on ourselves. Many times, we'd call in the air, thinking, *Maybe we can take some of those motherfuckers with us.* We were playing a real grown-up game out there, the object of which wasn't whether you lived or died but how you lived and how you died.

The average age of Marines in the bush in those days was eighteen. Most of us, like myself, had our nineteenth birthday over there. So when we were having dinner and shooting the shit, maybe sitting around the edge of our hole eating C rations, which had been heated if we were lucky or just cold out of the can, the conversation might turn to how many times a Marine had gotten laid. The answers were always lies. Or we might talk about how we wanted to die, which was something we all thought about a lot. "Well, I don't want to get burned, I know that," I would often say. None of us wanted to be burned, and none wanted to be captured. A lot of guys would say they didn't even want to be involved in the decision-making process at all—just make it quick. For me, that was a nightmare death, because I wanted to confront mine head-on. I never prayed to God not to die, as most guys did. For me, that seemed dishonorable. When I prayed, I prayed for two things: one, that I wouldn't let my buddies down and, two, that I'd have time to face my death. Later, as I lay bleeding out and dying, I was incredibly grateful to God for that opportunity. The worst type of death I could imagine, my greatest fear, was walking point, stepping on a booby trap, and, with one instant left in my life, seeing my buddy get vaporized, with only enough time left to say, "Oh, no."

The first time I saw combat with the NVA, it was baptism by fire. These guys were completely invisible. We could be eating bread off them and still couldn't see them, and they were firing full fucking automatic. They had AK-47s, SKSs, RPGs, and RPG-7s that fired B40 rockets. Meanwhile, the Marine Corps had taken away our 3.5-inch rocket launchers, or "super bazookas," and we had been given LAW rockets, which were 66-millimeter disposable light anti-tank rounds. It was basically a telescoping tube that dispatched a rocket. You'd pull a pin on it and pop off the end, and when you reached up and squeezed the trigger mechanism, which was supposed to send an electrical charge to arm the rocket, and it didn't work, then you had a useless armed rocket launcher with you. And you couldn't leave it, because if you did, the NVA would use it. They'd turn it into a booby trap that would kill another Marine. So you had to hang on to the son of a bitch, which was really fucking awkward, because you might be carrying up to three of them. Like their AK-47s, they had this great rocket launcher, and we had this piece of shit that was just like our rifle, undependable.

When a bullet whizzes by you, traveling faster than sound, it doesn't go *doooing* or *kacthow,* as it does on TV. It makes a really loud "CRACK," and if it's really close to you, it stings, because that crack is a little sonic boom. It is traveling so quickly through the air that the air closes in behind it, and you hear CRACK, but by the time you hear it, it's either past you or in you. When a bullet travels by you so close it stings, there are no words to describe how terrifying that is. And the thing is, when you go to the ground in the bush, nobody can see you. What happens next, and whether you are going to do your job, is just between you and God. It's really hard to be brave when nobody is watching you. When someone is shooting at you, especially when he's close, it's easy to get very rational, and reason can make a coward of a man. When you're terrified and you want to live, it's only reasonable for you not to lift up your head or pick up your rifle and shoot back, so that people know exactly where you are, and then fire more in your direction. It's rational and logical, according to everything you've been raised to think, not to jump up and expose yourself in a firefight, even though that's what it's going to take to keep your buddies, and maybe even you, alive. When someone is hurt and screaming in the dark, it's only reasonable to think, *I can't help him if I'm dead or wounded. It's probably better for me to stay right here so the enemy doesn't know where I am.* Your mind can come up with all kinds of rationalizations for you not to do what a Marine should do in a firefight, and reason made a coward of me more times than I'd wish to admit. But the bravest things I ever did were when nobody could see them.

The NVA made contact only if they were sure they had the advantage. If you were in a squad, they would initiate only if they had a platoon. If you were in a platoon, then they'd have a company or a battalion. If you had a battalion, then they wouldn't make contact until they had a regiment. So whenever they did decide to hit us, they did it when they were very close and always when they wanted to initiate and not when we wanted them to initiate. Almost every major fight I was in with the NVA they initiated with an ambush. It was their fucking yard, and they were masters of the L shape and the horseshoe ambush. And when they hit us at night, North Vietnamese sappers, or combat engineers, could crawl silently through our razor wire and tangle-foot and through fields saturated with Bouncing Betty mines and toe poppers, and we wouldn't know they were there until they were inside the wire of our position, throwing hand grenades and satchel charges into our holes and bunkers. We called them ghosts and phantoms, and we meant it. To this day, I'm still afraid of the dark. Sometimes, we would find their bodies, and they would still be wearing loincloths. If they had been wearing uniforms, we would have seen them, but they stripped off their clothes, lubricated themselves by coating their skin in grease from head to toe, and slid through barbed wire and trip wires. They could somehow get through all of our defenses without being snagged. They'd also have tourniquets on each arm above the elbow, and on each leg above the knee, so that if they lost an extremity, they could cinch down the tourniquet and stay in the fight. That's hard-core. I was constantly stepping on barbed wire and trip wires as we were setting up, but those guys could somehow get through them without being snagged. We'd find boxes in the bush with their names on them, filled with hair clippings and fingernails. These were little sacrifice boxes, because they figured they were never going to return once they entered the perimeter, and so they wanted to leave something behind that could be sent home and buried. That's how committed they were, and that's what made them so frightening.

Every time we went out, we did so with equipment we couldn't trust, outnumbered by an enemy that was more motivated than we were, because they were fighting for their own cause in their own land. We were plenty motivated, too. Because the majority of us were volunteers and considered ourselves professional warriors, motivation was never a problem for us in 1967. But we felt as if the NVA had almost everything going their way, and that could be dispiriting at times. Because I shot my mouth off about being a point man, I would get told to walk point on a lot of patrols. And every time I walked point, I carried my rifle with the selector switch on rock and roll. I figured if I got hit, I'd need to lay down that first magazine of bullets on full auto to try to distract them. I always fixed my bayonet and had it ready in case my rifle didn't work, and I pulled out a hand grenade and kept it in easy reach. When walking point, I just expected to get hit, and the more I did it, the harder it became to shake the feeling that it was just a matter of time.

By late September, I quit marking my short-timer calendar, which most of us carried around to count down the days we had left on our deployment. I knew I wasn't going to make it, and every time I marked up the calendar, I felt like an idiot. Because of the casualties we had taken, our saying was "In 1-9, you're never short, you're always next." If you were short, it meant you were going home soon, but we could take no comfort in being short-timers, because we knew that the chances of our becoming casualties were very high. And most of us had already been wounded more than once. So the saying turned out to be true for me and for most of my buddies. When we went out on an operation, we were issued three C-ration meals, and we'd be told that a resupply would come every three days, conditions, circumstances, and weather permitting. An emergency resupply in combat is water and ammunition, things you can't live without, and nothing more. In the hot season in northern I Corps zone, the temperature got as hot as 130 degrees at 100 percent humidity. A human body will begin to dehydrate within a couple of hours in those conditions, and so water becomes the most essential supply in the field. The three nightmares in the bush were, in this order, your rifle not working, running out of ammo, and running out of water.

If you're supposed to be resupplied every three days, then what you would do on the first day was eat everything you didn't want to hump before you moved out of the perimeter. You had to figure out your food in three-day plans, unless you made contact or somebody got sick and you got an emergency resupply and maybe they'd be able to throw something onto the mede-vac for you—no guarantees—like a couple of five-gallon cans of water or sandbags full of shit C-ration meals nobody wanted in the rear. We'd take them and we'd eat them in the bush, even if they were crap. When you're starving, you find out that you're a lot more open-minded about what you eat. I lost thirty-three pounds in the bush. We lived with such a short-range outlook that if we ever ran out of water during the dry, hot season and we found a bomb crater filled with filthy, stagnant water so thick that you would have to press two fingers over the opening of your canteen to strain out the chunks, we would drink that fucking water, knowing that we were going to get sick. The question was simply when. We'd ask the corpsman, and he'd say probably forty-eight hours. "Well, fuck that, Doc," we'd reply. "We don't know if we'll be here in forty-eight hours. We're thirsty now." U.S. troops at Tarawa, Iwo Jima, and Peleliu had all faced similar conditions—the agony and desperation of not having water in temperatures in excess of a hundred degrees and 100 percent humidity. Having joined their ranks, we were beyond thirsty and completely disinterested in talking about the future, because we knew we didn't have one.

Part of the burden of being a survivor is that I discarded my future pretty early in the bush. I realized my future was nothing more than a pipe dream, and if you lived for your future or some fantasy of what it might be, you were not going to do anything to jeopardize it, which meant you were not going to do everything your buddies needed you to do in a firefight. All the hope of having a future does is slow you down. In combat, it's best to throw it away. So I discarded the concept of a future, and once you do that, it's difficult to ever reclaim it.

When I survived the war and finally made it home—try as I did—I couldn't make myself unthink that the future was bullshit, a fucking pipe dream, and it was never real to me again, until I had my first child in 1984. That was the moment when I began to believe in a future again, for the first time since returning from Vietnam. It was a future worth fighting for, and it belonged to my son. I ended up having other children, and they all had futures, which were more important than anything in my life, and they helped me to believe in the future even more. But for all those years after I came home and before they were born, if I had money, I spent it. If I had food, I ate it, just like in the bush, when I was told I'd be walking point and had been saving a can of peaches in my cargo pocket. I'd say, "Hold on a minute," and I'd immediately open that fucking can of peaches and snarf it down right there, because I didn't want the NVA to go through my pockets and take my peaches or eat my pound cake. Peaches and pound cake was my favorite C-ration dessert. It wasn't meant to be a dessert—the peaches were packed separately from the pound cake—but the bush taught us to be creative when it came to cuisine.

CHAPTER 8

M-I-S-E-R-Y

Me in a poncho and helmet at Camp Carroll,
just south of the DMZ, during monsoon season.

DURING MY TIME IN VIETNAM, I learned to spell infantry M-I-S-E-R-Y. That's what we called it. Our helmets were our billboards, and I'd written on the back of mine, "Missouri is the state I'm from, but misery is the state I'm in." We were always hungry in the bush, and we were always thirsty, except during the monsoon season, but then we'd be freezing our asses off. We'd get immersion foot, a condition that develops when feet are kept wet in soggy or muddy boots for days. When the outer layer of skin absorbs enough water, it begins to rot off, which made it almost impossible to keep flesh on our feet. And we were in the infantry, so we walked everywhere, which meant you would be walking on raw meat, and you wouldn't get to take your boots off very often, because a barefoot American is a defenseless American. One of the first things the North Vietnamese would do when they captured an American was take away his boots, because they knew we couldn't handle the bush barefoot and they could. By the time you finally got a chance to take off your boots, your socks came off in strips, and chunks of socks would be stuck inside your boots, and parts of socks would be stuck to sores on your feet. You had to peel them off, which meant opening the wounds anew. One of the things that a couple of my buddies and I would do every morning was see who could drain the most pus out of their jungle-rot ulcers.

Out in the bush our utility trousers rotted off, from the knees up, across the groin, down to the other knee, because we sweated so much. And whenever we were wet, everything ended up in the groin area. It wouldn't dry well, and so the seams there would give way first. We didn't wear underwear in the bush, because if you did, it would give you horrible rashes, rashes that would turn into pus-filled sores from jungle rot. So you learned pretty quick, don't wear Skivvies in the bush, and you'd tell your new guys as soon as they got there, "Take those Skivvies off and use 'em for shit paper because they're going to hurt you if you keep wearing them." In every C-ration meal, you would get a tiny packet of semi-water-resistant toilet paper, about the size of a pack of cigarettes, which was right on the edge of worthless; it felt like wiping your ass with wax paper.

So the Skivvies, which were made of absorbent cloth, came in handy for at least one use as shit paper, but if you wore them as clothing, they trapped moisture and hastened jungle rot. When your groin is exposed to nature and everything in it, you are going to catch things there. Every bandolier of ammunition would come with one black safety pin on it. I took to saving those safety pins, so I could try to pin my trousers closed when they would rot. The problem with rotting cloth is you can run a pin through it, but then the cloth will give way around the pin, so you were constantly adjusting to keep your trousers from rotting off.

We were always hungry and thirsty in the bush, and we always had diarrhea. And if you scratched a mosquito bite, in twenty-four hours you would have a pus-filled sore. The mosquitoes were so thick and big over there that we had a joke that mosquitoes in Vietnam were big enough to stand flat-footed on a rice paddy and fuck a turkey in his ass. That's teenage grunt humor for you. The mosquitoes were huge, and the female anopheles mosquito was the one that gave you malaria. It would stick its back legs in the air and spread them when it bit you. So we called it being bitten by the bitch or by the whore. If you were lucky you had insect repellent, but you weren't always lucky. And because the repellent would keep them only about an inch away from you and they were so loud, hovering that close to your head and buzzing like crazy, you would get scared that you would not hear the enemy. Sometimes, after falling asleep at night, you would wake up with so many mosquito bites on your hands that you'd have to work your fingers in order to bend them, or your lips and eyelids, which were soft and filled with blood, would swell up to twice their size, punctured by dozens of bites.

There are a few things that a grunt in Asia learns to hate: mosquitoes, because they're so big; rats, as big as Shetland ponies, because they live off corpses; and leeches, because you can't keep them off you and they're bloodsucking parasites. There would be times when I'd have twenty leeches on me at once. I've had guys tell me they've had more than thirty, because when they attached to you, you couldn't stop to remove them. You had to keep doing your job. A lot of guys said they never felt them, but I could feel them when they latched on and it hurt.

The leeches would attach themselves all over you. They'd attach to your armpits. They'd congregate in the groin. They'd burrow into your scalp. (They liked areas where there was some pressure.) They'd get inside your waistband, latch on, and then they'd excrete an anticoagulant so your blood wouldn't harden up and it would continue to flow.

If you managed to get one off, you'd have a big bleeding hole where the leech had been, and by the time you'd walked ten meters, there would be another leech back on that same hole. You never got one leech; you'd be covered in them. And when you finally stopped long enough to take your insect repellent and squirt them, they'd drop off right away, but it was like pouring salt on an open wound. Some guys would light a cigarette and burn them off, and that was real effective if you were in a place where you could take a chance on the smell of a cigarette. A cigarette could be smelled a long way off and would serve as a warning that somebody was nearby. Tigers and monkeys don't smoke cigarettes. So when you smelled a cigarette and it wasn't from someone smoking nearby, it usually meant danger. So you couldn't always light a cigarette, but when you could, you'd get all the leeches off and then you would have all these open wounds that wouldn't scab and would just keep bleeding. They would climb onto your testicles, and you'd burn them off, and the blood would be flowing from there, and you'd go back to work and try concentrating on your job because you wanted to live another day.

We were running an operation, a platoon-size operation. I'm pretty sure we were southwest of Khe Sanh, and we were told that we were close to the Laotian border. At night, we wanted to get our platoon base on high ground. It gave us the advantage to be able to shoot down on the enemy, and it made the enemy work harder to get to us, because they had to compete against gravity. So we found a hill and dug in. It was evening, and the difference between evening and night in the jungle is pretty damn small. The whole platoon needed water, so the lieutenant sent us out on water detail. We got six men with ropes, and each man in the platoon could send two of his canteens down. There were around thirty of us in the platoon, so we had nearly sixty canteens strung out between six guys, which would be a lot of water, and would be pretty heavy once they were filled. We descended the hill into the lowlands, where our map showed there was a water source. We were operating in very low light condition, and when we reached the water source, we discovered it was a swamp. Nothing good ever happens in a swamp.

There were two of us with rifles, and I was on point. The guys with the canteens were just carrying pistols. So this was not a heavily armed patrol. When I reached the swamp, I saw that it was all covered with jungle growth, and I was looking from very low light into even lower light. When you walk point, you walk with all of your senses, like tentacles protruding from all over your body, sniffing at the air, trying to get a taste of what was going on, your sense of smell, your sense of taste, your hearing, however damaged it might have been from the many firefights you had been in. So all of my senses were cranked to ten as I approached that swamp, walking point, when, all of a sudden, I had this feeling, like when you are walking through a crowd and you feel somebody looking at you. One of the things you learn from the old-timers, and one of the first things you tell new men when they come aboard, is that if you are close to the enemy, never look at them, because if you look at them, they'll look at you. They will feel the energy coming out of your eyes. We were taught to look over their shoulders, because you could see everything they do with your peripheral vision.

Suddenly I had the feeling that something was wrong. I couldn't put my finger on it, but before I stepped into that undergrowth and into the swamp, I dropped to a knee and held up my left fist, the sign of danger. The longer I knelt there, the more vulnerable I felt, because I was staying in one place and giving these guys a lot of time to put their sights right on my chest. But I had to figure this out. We needed that water. We just had to have it. And as I was kneeling there reasoning with myself, it dawned on me what was wrong. Everything in the overgrowth of swamp looked blurry, as if I couldn't focus my vision on it. *What's wrong with me?* I thought. *Am I getting sick? Is this the first sign of malaria? Am I dehydrated?* As I was going through this catalog in my brain, I scooted a little closer to the swamp. All my senses were screaming, "Danger, Will Robinson! Danger, danger!" And then I realized what it was. Suddenly everything came into clear focus. Every leaf on every piece of growth in front of me was moving, or rather what was on it was moving. When tree leeches and ground leeches sense your body heat, they will stand erect on their bases and begin to move their heads around, wiggling and moving them, trying to locate the blood that is causing your body heat. What I was looking at were leeches covering every leaf and covering the ground, and there were water leeches, too, which would jump on us as soon as we stepped into the swamp.

We were going to have to crouch in the middle of this forest of leeches and fill all of the canteens. I signaled to the other guy, and he was scared because he knew something was wrong. I had been sitting still for too long. He scooted up to me and said, "What's the matter?" "Leeches," I replied, "thousands of leeches." He looked around and saw what I was referencing, and we both went, "Aw, fuck." I told him to spread the word, and he told the next guy, and the next told the next guy, until everybody was going. "Aw, fuck!" And then we had to walk in there. Of course, by the time I got close enough to see them, I was already fucked. So we went in there, and it was getting dark, and the guys had to put these canteens in the water, holding their fingers over the canteens to hopefully catch any water leeches before they slithered into the canteens, which slowed the process of filling all those fucking canteens.

We got all of the canteens filled and strung between the six guys, and we were getting ready to move, when some NVA showed up on the other side of the swamp. I guess they were there for the same reason we were. They needed water, and there was an exchange of fire. For myself and the other rifleman, our only reason to exist at that moment was to protect the water. The platoon needed it, so we sent the other guys booking for the top of the hill, and then we turned back to do a leapfrog, when one guy stopped and the other guy ran around him and then stopped, so the other guy could run around him. We knew that if the NVA were pursuing us, we'd have to stop and light them up as we were leapfrogging, always with a rifle pointed downrange at the enemy. We could hopefully move back to safety that way, but we knew we couldn't move faster than the guys with the water, because we were the firepower for the water detail, and we had to protect them. As I ran past the other rifleman, my Saint Christopher was bouncing on my chest on my dog tag chain. I kept my dog tags in my pocket because they made too much noise. The chain snagged on something, and I felt it snap. I spun around and dropped to the ground. *I had to find that Saint Christopher or I would die,* I thought. Mrs. Holcomb had gotten it blessed and had prayed over it, and it had become a symbol of divine protection to me. I wasn't leaving without it. I was convinced I would be killed without it, so I was more than willing to risk my life to find it.

The other kid came running to leapfrog me and saw me down on all fours, no longer pointing my rifle downrange, but digging through the foliage, looking for something. The grass was taller than we were, and the ground was covered with crushed grass where we had patrolled. Upon seeing me, he shouted, "Come on! Let's go! Let's go! Let's go!" And I said, "Go on! I'll be right behind you." "What's the matter?" he asked. When I told him, he said, "Fuck your Saint Christopher. We gotta go!" and I told him to go ahead again, but he wouldn't. He wouldn't leave me. And by the grace of God, the second time I stuck my hand on the ground, my Saint Christopher was in it. I couldn't see shit. My Saint Christopher could have landed just about anywhere after my chain snapped. The odds of my finding it in that foliage were about one in a fucking million. I looked at it and I thought, *Thank God,* and we both ran top speed up the side of that hill to join the water detail back at the platoon.

One of the worst things in the bush, on top of the sheer misery of the physical conditions, is the absolute terror of being on a night ambush or being assigned to a listening post. If you stared at a rock long enough in the dark, it would get up and move, and that would scare you damn near enough to make your heart stop. It was an illusion, but it still scared the shit out of me. For the listening post, they'd get three guys with a radio and send them as far as a thousand meters away, though we'd seldom ever go that far, even if we were told to go that far. They'd send us out of the perimeter and our job would be to listen for the enemy. There were several ways the unit would know if the enemy was out there. One was that we would hear the enemy and would have enough time to call in and warn that the enemy was coming. Then we'd ask for permission to come back inside the perimeter wire, and 99 percent of the time permission would be denied. Another was that the enemy would discover us, overrun us, and kill us, and that would notify the perimeter that the enemy was there. And finally there were the times when the enemy would be right next to us in the dark, so close that we could reach out and grab him, and even if we were able to somehow signal back to the unit they were there, we couldn't break contact because we were with the NVA. They would come so close some nights that we could hear them whispering to each other as they looked for us in the dark. You would be holding the handset to your ear really hard, because you were terrified that the CP, or command post, was going to call, having not heard from you in a while, and say, "Delta, Lima, Papa, three Bravo," which meant Delta company, listening post, Third Platoon, second squad. "If your sit rep is alpha sierra, key your handset twice. If your situation report is all secure, break, squelch twice on the handset." And if you can't make a sound, they might keep thinking you're asleep, so they would keep asking you if your sit rep is alpha sierra. But then it would finally dawn on them, maybe there was somebody too close for you to say anything. So then they would say, "If your sit rep is negative alpha sierra, key your handset once," and you damn near squeezed the handle off the handset, and you knew that if you didn't hold that handset up to your ear hard enough the NVA, who were close enough that you could hear them whispering, would hear the radio, and then you would be as good as dead.

So when you got a listening post, you felt as if you were getting a death sentence, and in the bush you'd get one two or three times a week. It was terrifying shit. There wasn't a moment when I was in the bush, especially when I was in 1-9, when I wasn't scared to death. Most of the time I was scared senseless. In Vietnam, we measured fear on a scale called the pucker factor. We discovered that our assholes puckered when we were scared, so the pucker factor was devised as a way to communicate our fear level to another Marine. The best pucker factor report I ever heard was when a buddy declared that he was so scared you couldn't ram a "straight pin up my ass with a sledge hammer." The pucker factor was on a scale of one to ten, but there were times when your pucker factor would be a twenty. A guy might tell you, "The pucker factor was so bad it turned me inside out," and you know he was fucking terrified. We were dealing in ultimate realities out there on the listening posts, and there always came a point at which we were no longer dealing with reality. Reality was dealing with us.

CHAPTER 9

Operation Buffalo

Con Thien, fall of 1967, taken during the siege.
Left to right: Sam Tatum, Dan Cooney, and Corporal Bourne.
The last Marine's name is unknown; he was killed shortly after this
photo was taken. The other three were wounded at Khe Sanh.

WE CALLED OUR STAY at Con Thien, that three-top hill just south of the DMZ, "time in the barrel." We were the fish. The NVA had the shotguns. They stuck them in the barrel and blasted away. Without fail, they hit something with every shot. Con Thien was such a small area that it was constantly getting pounded with artillery from North Vietnam, only two miles away. They simply couldn't miss. Marines in the Third Marine Division in northern I Corps in the spring and summer of 1967 called the DMZ the Dead Marine Zone, because we lost so many of our men up there. Our unit had suffered so many casualties on and around Con Thien in a series of battles and sweeps that we began to think Delta Company was doomed. That's how we got the name the Walking Dead, or Dying Delta.

On the morning of July 2, 1967, the 1-9 Marines had commenced Operation Buffalo, a sweep of an area at the southern edge of the DMZ in which two companies—Alpha and Bravo— were ambushed by the NVA. Bravo Company was overrun, fired upon from three sides, and almost completely wiped out. Thirty mortar rounds came raining down upon them in less than three minutes. Alpha Company, which had been sent to rescue the survivors from Bravo, was soon pinned down and gutted. The only unit that 1-9 had left to send out as a reaction force was the Third Platoon of Delta Company, my unit, and we were totally underresourced.

I remember fewer than thirty of us climbing onto the backs of four tanks and riding toward the DMZ. Though we knew what we were getting into, not one of us hesitated. We were terrified, yes. But those were our buddies out there getting killed, and we were Marines. We couldn't leave them out there. If all we could do was die with them, that was what we would do, but we weren't going to abandon our friends.

In the distance, we heard one of the biggest firefights of our lives. The radiomen were telling us about the things that were coming over the radio, and they weren't good. The fighting was just beyond the firebreak, or the McNamara Line, and we could hear Bravo Company getting slaughtered, because one of the radiomen had a speaker on his radio and he cranked it up. There were kids dying on the radio, and there was one kid out there who was holding the transmit switch and begging them to come and help him, saying, "Everybody's dead. Please come and get me. Please help me. Help me. Help!" and he wouldn't let go of the transmit switch. So when he finally broke squelch, we knew he was dead.

We did our best to clear a helicopter-landing zone so we could evacuate the wounded. We weren't even trying to get the dead out at that point. There were just too many of them. It turned out to be one of the worst days for the U.S. Marines in Vietnam. We evacuated 166 wounded and managed to recover 51 dead, but we left behind 34 dead Marines, many of whom had been executed at close range, shot in the face or the back of the head, when their M16s jammed.

Time and *Newsweek* ran articles with photos from that fight, with pictures of those dead Marines from Bravo Company stacked up like wood, like trash, on the backs of the tanks. We couldn't get to them quick enough to save them. But while we were out there, our platoon commander was wounded, and he jumped on a helicopter and flew away. Then our platoon sergeant got hit. He was screaming horribly, but the corpsmen couldn't do anything, and he died. One guy went nuts and took off, running all the way through Con Thien screaming, "Everybody's dead. Everybody's getting killed!" First they wiped out our platoon leadership. Then, a couple of days later, a 152-millimeter artillery round landed right on top of Captain Richard Sasek and First Sergeant Jettie Rivers, killing them both, decapitating our company, and taking away the two men who made us feel as if we had any chance of getting home. We all respected the hell out of First Sergeant Rivers. He was the youngest first sergeant in the Marine Corps, but he was a bad son of a bitch, and we felt proud to be under his leadership. He had already been offered a commission, and he told them, "Hell no," he was going to be "the youngest sergeant major in the Marine Corps." He was black, and he was even harder on black Marines than on white ones. He'd say, "There are only two colors in this Marine Corps, red and forest green. Forest green is the color of our uniform, and red is the color of our blood. Ain't no other colors." First Sergeant Rivers earned the Navy Cross for valor in May 1967, for always staying with us in the field and going through the fights with us.

A day or so later, another artillery round landed on the doorway of the battalion command post. Boom. They decapitated the battalion. I was told after the fight that if you had put the survivors of Alpha Company, Delta Company, and Charlie Company together, you wouldn't have one rifle company all told. That's how badly we were hurt.

The new first sergeant who replaced Rivers was a complete coward. He treated us like shit. During the monsoon season, when they threw us back to the rear on three days' rest, he made grunts who had been out in the bush for months come inside his tent and dig a hole for him to hide in, next to his rack, so he wouldn't get wet in the monsoon. We hated him for it, and while I never saw anybody get fragged while I was in Vietnam—there were at least seven hundred documented cases of fragging during the war, in which lower enlisted troops deliberately killed officers or noncommissioned officers—we took up a collection for that guy. Nobody ever cashed it in, but I certainly thought about it. He was what we called a chicken fucker.

Then our new captain, from "Eighth & I," or Marine Barracks Washington, D.C., the home of the Marine Corps commandant, came right in and started insulting us. The 1-9 had just been decimated, and he called us crybabies because we were mourning our dead. When we tried to explain to him why his orders weren't good orders and that he was going to get us killed, he called us cowards. This is probably what hurt the most, to not be allowed to grieve. But we didn't have a choice. All we could do was suck it up and move on, and that's exactly what we did.

In September 1967, the NVA began their bombardment of Con Thien, shelling us with more than two hundred artillery and mortar rounds a day, peaking on September 25, when more than twelve hundred mortar rounds struck the base in a single day. This period marked the beginning of the siege, and during the fall of 1967 it seemed the shelling would never end. The siege took place during the monsoon, and so the conditions for the fighting were especially challenging. The NVA had cut off our supply route, and it was difficult to get aerial resupply and air support, and those were the two things we had that they didn't. The NVA had resolved to test us—possibly as a rehearsal for the upcoming siege of Khe Sanh in January 1968, which tactically served as a diversion for the Tet Offensive—to see how far we'd go to hold the position. We were getting newspaper clippings from our families back home that referred to Con Thien as the Alamo, and we were the Davy Crockett generation, so we sure as hell knew what that meant. We were told that we were surrounded by three NVA divisions. We didn't know if this was going to be an all-out attack in which they would try to take the position, or if they would hold us in place and try to starve us out, or if the United States would go all in to protect the position. But those of us who were there at that time were convinced the NVA planned to overrun us. We were certain of it.

It was bad enough being constantly bombarded by NVA artillery and mortars, but on Friday, October 13, we were attacked by our own fighter jets. It had been an unusually clear day, and it was an especially clear night, with a big moon, what my World War II father called "a bomber's moon." Around 9:00 p.m. that night, right out of the blue, two Marine Phantoms bombed my platoon. A five-hundred-pound bomb dropped directly on our CP, or command post, bunker, blowing away the wire in front of our position. No one knew what had hit us. We thought it had come from enemy aircraft. And I remember enormous amounts of dirt raining down upon us. Afraid that I was going to be buried, I got up on my hands and knees at the bottom of my hole as the dirt kept falling in on me. In the midst of the chaos, I immediately started trying to figure out who was hit by looking at who was standing around. *How many of our guys are left?* I wondered, trying to assess who had been in the CP bunker. Then I heard the screams coming out of the hole where the CP bunker had once been, and knew I couldn't go in and see who was making those sounds. In the end, four Marines died, and the rest who were in the CP bunker had to be medevaced out because of their injuries. The person I was closest to who died in the CP bunker that night was a Navy corpsman named George Shade. He was from Pennsylvania and never let us down. I liked him a lot and was pretty devastated when he died. It seemed like such a waste to survive Operation Buffalo, only to be killed by our own jets. Dan Cooney went into the ruins of the bunker and brought Doc out.

The next day, I wrote a letter to my father recounting what had happened, in which I said,

The thing that gets me, Dad, is that there was no excuse for it at all. They had a "bomber's moon," nearly completely full, with visibility outstanding. . . . I can't understand how they could do it and I'll never be able to forgive these Pilots for what they've done. . . . It's the most horrible thing in the world to be on the receiving end of an air strike. There is no more helpless feeling in the world than when you know it's your own planes doing it. . . . I'll never cheer another airstrike again, even though it's against the gooks. I know what they're going through and I don't wish it on anybody. When I see one now all I do is shudder and say a simple little prayer. "God have mercy on us all, and help bring this war to an end." Every Marine that's left in Delta Co., 3rd Plt. says much the same prayer also. Take care and don't worry about me, because I'm fine. Pray for peace. Don't worry because God is with me. Your Loving Son, John.

After we were bombed by our own jets—the greatest betrayal—I lost what little faith I had left in the war. I never lost my faith in the Corps, but I no longer believed in what we were doing on that little mound of dirt two miles south of the

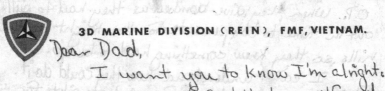

3D MARINE DIVISION (REIN), FMF, VIETNAM.

Dear Dad,

    I want you to know I'm alright. It's by the grace of God that myself and the other men left in my platoon are alive now.

    On Friday the 13th of Oct. we got hit in the most horrible way: by our own jets. It was around 9 P.M. I think, when they attacked. There was two of them and they dropped 8 or 9, 250 pound and 500 pound bombs in our platoon area. They hit our platoon C.P. bunker and wiped out our C.P. group. It's a miracle that there were only 4 killed. Every man in our C.P. group was wounded seriously enough that they had to be medevaced. The only man that didn't get hit in our C.P. group was our new Lt. and he was out checking the lines when they hit.

    The thing that gets me, Dad, is there was no excuse for it at all. They had a "bombers moon" nearly completely full, with visibility outstanding. The perimeter of Con Thien has been here, manned by Marines for over 6 months and the terrain features are unmistakable. Con Thien is 3 hills on an open area. They are the only 3 hills in a very large area which is the reason we're here, it's an Arty

O.P. When they dive-bombed us they had to pull out in time to compensate for the height of the hills, so they knew something had to be up.

I can't understand how they could do it and I'll never be able to forgive these pilots for what they've done. Digging out the dead and wounded from the C.P. bunker hurt me bad because everyone of them was my buddies. Half of the men were buried alive in their fighting holes and it was a fight against time to locate the holes and dig them out before a man could suffocate, luckily we did.

"Doc" Shade, the Corpsman who ran from his well protected position to my little hole to treat me on the 27th of August when I got hit, was killed. He was in the C.P. bunker.

I took over Herbies M-60 machine-gun, he was killed also, and set it in position. The gooks hit us, as we knew they would when they realized what was happening. They didn't get through us. I was a gunner all night but gave it to "Porky" in the morning. Thank God there wasn't too many of them.

You can't even recognize our area now. It's all different, with 20 foot deep craters all over the place, pushing the dirt up into new hills.

It's the most horrible thing in the world to be on the recieving end of an air strike. There is no more helpless feeling in the world than when you know it's your own planes doing it.

I don't think they'll ever tell you all in the states what happened. Some of the newspaper articles some of the guys have recieved from home on Con Thien have sounded like they're not talking about the same place we're at. If they didn't tell about us getting hit by our own planes, don't tell Mom. I'm fine except for my nerves which are a little goofed up now. God was with us all Dad and his hand covered me that night. I came out without a scratch.

If I thought it would do any good I'd write Jack Gant or Symington or LBJ but what could they do. The damage has been done, they can't bring anyone back, all they could do is bring us home and I don't think too many us would leave.

Just want you to know I'm alright and everything is fine now. The gooks still arty the crap out of us but we're used to that. After what we've been through now even artillery seems small. I can now say I've been through everything that's been in this war.

I don't think they'll ever make that mistake again, I pray they won't. I'll never cheer another airstrike again, even though it's against the gooks. I know what they're going through and I don't wish it on anybody. When I see one now all I do is shudder and say a simple little prayer.

"God have mercy on us all, and help bring this war to an end."

Every Marine thats left in "Delta Co., 3rd Plt., says much the same prayer also.

Take care and don't worry aboutme, because I'm fine. Pray for peace.

Don't worry because God is with me.

Your Loving Son,

John

P.S. "I've heard of "close air support" but that was ridiculous.

DMZ, getting shelled and bombed by our enemies as well as our friends. It was then that I could no longer ignore the thought that had been nagging at me for months. *Why were we here?*

On November 1, Delta Company was tasked with the first offensive action in Con Thien since the siege had begun in early September. Jim Rye was my fire team leader. I'd known him since infantry training, and he was the best point man in the fucking world as far as I was concerned. I learned a lot from him and always tried to be as slow and as methodical as he was whenever I walked point. Neither Jim nor I would ever be rushed, even if the officers told us to speed it up, because we knew that rushing was how mistakes got made and how our friends would be left exposed and unsafe. So we took a lot of shit for it. They called us Turtle Rye and Snail Musgrave because of the way we walked point, to which we would always fire back that we were happy to be point men who still had both of their legs.

By that point, we never had a full squad. The most we had was ten guys, but on the day in question, when our company was sent into an NVA battalion area, we had only seven. So we broke into two fire teams. It was our fire team's turn to lead the squad. And Jim looked at me and said to take point on our fire team. I returned his stare, trying not to telegraph my feelings, and thought, *Holy shit, Jim, what have you done? You are killing me, here.* None of us wanted to walk point on that patrol, because we all knew that we were hanging well off the end of a branch by our fingernails and there were all kinds of buzz saws out there waiting to cut us down. Though it was one of the most intense patrols I'd ever walked point on, it wasn't eventful, thank God.

Then the bird dog—or forward air controller that flew over areas to look for targets—came in over the radio and passed the word that there were beaucoup NVA advancing on us at double time, and he suggested we pick up our marbles and go home. I mean, there were no two ways about it. We were getting the fuck out of there right away. We weren't retreating, but we tried to exit stage left at a pretty good clip. The NVA numbers were so large that B-52s were redirected to our position as the NVA converged and tried to pin us down. We were the ultimate bait out there, a Marine company that had the potential to get their asses handed to them and maybe even get wiped out. The enemy knew we would draw all kinds of other units to us, and so they were mobilizing quickly to corner us. It was pretty intense as we raced back to base. We were the last squad of the last platoon out there, and we were firing rockets in the general direction of the NVA, with the belief that there were so many targets out there that one of the rockets was bound to hit. Plus we wanted to get rid of those rockets, because they were so fucking awkward and heavy. Fortunately, we made it back in time and no one was hurt.

Five nights later, on November 6, leadership came down and told us we were going out the next day on a two-company sweep. And as soon as they gave word that we were going out, I knew that was it. I just knew. I no longer thought I was going to get killed. I was sure of it, and I visualized my parents opening the envelope and reading the letter I had written to them in the event of my death, and I couldn't get the image out of my head. So I burned the letter. I didn't write to my girlfriend, Karen, either, because I somehow sensed by the tone of her letters that she was no longer committed to our relationship. But I did write to my friend Pat Van Buren's sister and thanked her for taking the time to write to me and for all the things she'd sent, telling her she had been a wonderful pen pal. I closed by saying that she didn't need to worry about writing anymore, because in the morning it would be done.

I spent the rest of the evening preparing myself for what was to come. I did a lot of praying and asked God to be with me and to carry me home. I said how grateful I was for the time I'd had, for all my friends, and I prayed that I would be the only one to get hit. I stayed up late, thinking over my life, knowing how hard the news was going to be on my family. But I had no regrets that night. There was never a moment when I asked, "Why the fuck did I do this? Why did I enlist, when I could be hiding out on a college campus, like most of my high school friends?" I never thought any of that. There was never any question in my mind. If I had to choose between dying in Vietnam, no matter how senseless the war had become, or thriving back home while other young men my age were shipped off to die, I would have chosen the former every time. But it wasn't a choice. This is what I had been called to do, my duty as a citizen. I knew going into the Marine Corps that this could always happen. I'd been lucky to come from such a wonderful and loving family, to have made so many good friends, the ones back home and my buddies in the Corps. I felt profound gratitude for all that I had been given and prayed that I wouldn't shame myself or let down any of my buddies. And then, all of a sudden, it was zero dark thirty. It was time to go.

CHAPTER 10

The Kill Zone

Photo of my buddies, including Jim Rye in the lower left,
whom my son Rye is named after. Jim helped save my life that last day.
Delta 1-9 in 1967 at Dong Ha.

W E HAD TO MOVE OUT through the minefield on the northern side. The gate to the path was right near my hole. It was by no means straight, because it had been designed to confuse the enemy. So we needed someone who knew the way to lead us. And I was really nervous because a week prior a fire team had gotten lost trying to do the same thing, navigating the minefield. It was so dark that they had been holding on to each other's belts, and not able to see anything, one of them stepped on a Bouncing Betty, right near my hole, and a fireball exploded, startling those of us nearby. I grabbed my rifle and hellbox and shouted, "Gooks in the wire!" I don't know what kept me from squeezing off both, but right after the mine went off, it was completely silent, and there was a brief, pregnant pause, during which we heard these guys moaning. One of them called out for his mother. Another cried out to God. Two of them were already dead. The other was suffering. I didn't have to see them, thank God, but I had to listen to their moans, and it was unbearable. Sloan, a young black Marine from the Deep South who had been given a choice by a judge to either go to jail for two years or join the Corps, and who later received the Silver Star, was the hero that night, along with Lieutenant Magee and a couple of corpsmen, who crawled out into that minefield to get the bodies of the two who were already dead and get the suffering one back inside the wire, but I didn't budge or volunteer to go out there. I was too scared of the mines. I stayed right where I was. The third kid ended up dying anyway, and it was torture to witness it and not be able to stop it.

Only days later, we were the ones going out there in the dark, down the same path on which those guys got lost. We lined up asshole to belly button, the entire company strung out single file, because the path through the minefield was very narrow, and some kid in one of the squads in one of the other platoons accidentally discharged his M79 grenade launcher. As soon as it fired, we all started debating which way the grenade had gone, because we hadn't been able to tell. When we learned it had fired straight up, we went down in unison with a collective "Aw, shit." I pushed my helmet back to cover as much of the back of my head as I could and simultaneously pulled up my flak jacket, so as to cover my neck and the base of my spine, fighting with myself over which way the grenade would land. It takes these things a long time to detonate. The M79 is a high-angle weapon with a long trajectory. I didn't know what range it had, so I just had to wait this thing out with all of the other guys. Forty-five seconds later—which seemed to take a day—it came down and, fortunately, landed about a hundred yards away. We all breathed a sigh of relief and started heading out into the field, thinking, *This cannot be good.*

Because of our little outing six days before, we knew how many NVA were out there. We knew for sure that two companies were not going to impress them and that they weren't going to pack up and start running home because of us. We moved out, heading northwest toward the hedgerows out in the field. Dawn was starting to break, and all of a sudden we saw people, about a hundred meters away. We pulled back and said, "Holy shit," thinking them to be NVA. We had an officer with us, a nice new guy, and it was his first patrol. He'd only been in country three weeks and had never been outside the wire. He yelled out, "Hey, buddy! We're over here! Delta Company right over here!" Of course, the guys we saw in the distance naturally turned around and started running for the hedges, and we simply could not believe the stupidity of this dumb-ass rookie move by this young officer. The explosion from the M79 grenade launcher could have been anything. It probably didn't sound the alarms. But now the NVA had made direct eye contact with us and then heard us yell at them that we were "Delta Company right over here!" I had already foreseen my own death the night before, and so this felt as if someone had placed a giant rock on my shoulders, and it was weighing me down even more. All of the signs were pointing in the wrong direction. It was clearly going to be a long, bad day, and I figured I wouldn't be the only one to go down.

By the time we got to the hedgerows, the sun had fully risen, and Third Platoon was on the right flank as we moved deeper into the foliage, overgrown rice paddies that grew thicker until we stumbled upon some kind of bunker. Our machine gun team leader, Corporal Beck, who was completely hard-core, went down and fragged it. There was nothing inside, but he fragged it for good measure, just to be safe. He had to run out in the open to do it, and that took balls, of which Corporal Beck had no shortage.

Suddenly we started taking fire. The kid right next to me, a new kid, got shot through the ankle. The three NVA who kept shooting at us really weren't aiming, but they managed to hit the kid anyway. That's when I knew it was going to happen. It was a favorite NVA trick, a tactic that was older than Custer. They sent a few guys out to draw you closer and then attacked. These guys were showing themselves, firing off a magazine, and then moving deeper into the bush. We kept telling our lieutenant, the same young officer who had yelled out to the NVA from the hedgerows, "Don't do this. These guys are just bait for a trap. Don't fall for this." But he was wet behind the ears and didn't understand what was happening. He got on the horn and called the new captain, the one who had called us crybabies. We didn't trust him, because he was a glory hound who had been heard openly talking about how he wanted to be highly decorated and we were going to be the tools for his advancement. So our lieutenant had his radioman call, "Delta Six Actual," which was the call sign for the captain. He related the situation—that we were taking fire from three NVA, who were moving deeper into the bush—and Delta Six Actual said, "I want their bodies. Bring me their bodies!" That's when those of us who knew what was going on looked at each other and said, "That's it."

Our lieutenant was a good guy, but he was out of his depth, and he had this overbearing captain telling him to get his ass out there, be aggressive, and get these guys who were shooting at us. Because we had received direct orders, there was no way around it, no possibility of saying no, even if the orders were without merit and would ultimately cost lives. This was the chain of command. It was designed to maintain order and discipline, but under bad leadership it could cause unnecessary death, chaos, and confusion. I didn't take it personally. We all work under bad leaders at one point or another in our lives. It's just that the stakes of what we were doing were life and death.

The young lieutenant was going to do what he was told, and it would lead to our demise, and eventually to his. It wasn't his fault; he was just new. The lieutenant and the captain died together at Khe Sanh, struck by the same round, which, in the end, was a shame, because they weren't all that bad. They had learned from their previous mistakes. But now they had fallen for the oldest NVA tactic, which was perfectly executed, because it pulled us off the flank, deeper and deeper into the bush. Why deal with three platoons when you can sucker one away and deal with it individually? It will be much easier to wipe out. We kept moving farther and farther away from the other platoons, as if the NVA had us on a leash and were just pulling us along, and as we went deeper, we just gritted our teeth and got our gear ready. I pulled out an extra magazine and a frag, praying that my rifle would work when I went to fire it. Just before we rolled out, I saw Lieutenant Magee, our former platoon commander, a seasoned leader whom we all respected, unlike our new lieutenant, who was placed right out of basic school. We knew Magee had our best interest in mind. He came over, slapped me on the shoulder, and said, "Keep it together now, Musgrave." He said my name and looked right at me, and it helped pump me up.

We hit the ground and kept driving on, deeper into the heavy foliage. In the thick of the growth, I couldn't see anyone, and it felt as if the whole war were directed at me. There was a lot of shit coming in, which clearly wasn't from the three guys anymore. With every step we took as we pursued them, the pucker factor ratcheted up higher. I felt myself clenching all of my muscles involuntarily, holding everything in, staying as close to Jim as I could while being tactically responsible, so they wouldn't get us both at the same time. I had absolute faith in Jim and always felt better if I was near him, because he handled everything so well. We were pretty close together when some of our guys started seeing people off in the foliage and began yelling, "Hey, look out!" We heard them calling back, "Hey, First Platoon, over here! Hey, buddy! Don't shoot!" It was the NVA. They were wearing Bravo Company's gear. They were in flak jackets and helmets and speaking in English.

Our grenadier was up ahead of us. He came around a corner and saw a Marine standing with his back to him, and he said, "Hey, buddy," and the guy turned around and he was NVA. And before our grenadier could react, the NVA shot him in the chest. He went down, and then the dance started. The sounds around us abruptly changed from individual shots to a roar as a hail of bullets and ordnance came raining down upon us. We were in the kill zone now. We immediately regrouped and tried to figure out how bad the situation was, where it was the worst, and what our orders were. I had no idea where the lieutenant or my good friend Leonard Blair was. All of a sudden somebody yelled out, "Blair's hit! Blair's hit bad!" and that scared me because Blair was my buddy. Sloan, one of the bravest enlisted men in the platoon, was Blair's best friend, and he went running after him, leaping over us and anything that got in his way, with his rifle out to one side, yelling, "I'm coming, Blair! I'm coming!" At this point it dawned on me: *Blair's my buddy, and I'm lying down out here hiding while Sloan is risking his life to save him. Get your head out of your ass, Musgrave. Blair is your friend. What the fuck are you doing?* So I picked myself up to run after Sloan. And that's when I got shot.

I didn't know it, because I didn't feel it. I was sprinting toward Sloan when the first round got me. It was a ricochet, which hit me on the left side of my chin, fractured my jaw, and left me unconscious. One minute I was up, and the next I was facedown on the ground, lying flat, with my right hand under my head. As with getting hit in the face with a baseball bat, there wasn't one point of pain, just a large area that hurt really bad. There was blood pouring down my arm, and somebody was yelling, "Are you all right? Are you all right?" and I honestly didn't know. "How bad are you hit?" he said, and I replied, "In the face or in the throat," and I tried to move but couldn't. I was stunned, scared stiff. But he, whoever he was, kept yelling to me and said, "I'm coming to get you." I had no idea how far he was from me, because it all happened so fucking fast.

Next thing I saw was a jungle boot slamming right next to my face. I could hear the other foot planting by my left shoulder, and I felt his hands come under my armpits and grab the front of my shoulders to pull me up. And when he pulled me up, the gunner who shot me the first time fired again. At least two rounds hit the ground in front of me. Now, the brain can do funny things when reacting to physical trauma. I was aware that he fired that first burst into me. At least two rounds hit in front of me, and then I took them in the chest. The rounds struck me before the sound of the gun reached my ear. I had been hurt a few times in my life, a couple of times seriously, but had never felt anything like that. The only analogy I have been able to come up with is that it felt as if I had been hit in the chest by a speeding train. I saw my shoulders slam together in front of my face. I know that's impossible, but that's what I saw. And there was this all-consuming fire of pain that swallowed me and enveloped my entire world.

When you were out in the bush and someone screamed, it was easy to tell the difference between someone who was scared and someone who'd been hit bad. There's both pain and terror in the scream when someone gets hit. Suddenly I heard someone screaming that way, and, God, it sounded so fucking horrible, and I couldn't figure out who it was. Then, an instant later, my mind caught up with my body, and I realized the scream was coming from me. I had dirt in my mouth, like when a dog is hit by a car and ends up in a ditch, snapping at everything. I thought, *I've been shot,* and then immediately shut up. I commanded myself to be quiet. *I'm going to die,* I thought, and suddenly I was okay. I made peace with it. I couldn't do anything about it. It was in God's hands now.

I was one of the first people from my company to get shot that day. As I understand it, both of our corpsmen were hit right away. I didn't see them get hit, but they must have been taken out quickly, because I wasn't attended to by a corpsman in the field. The NVA were always targeting our corpsmen for this reason. It happened so quickly. One round put me down. Our grenadier got hit at the same time, shot through the right side of his chest.

It's well known that Marines never leave their dead, and they never ever leave their wounded. It's not a slogan. This is a tremendous comfort when you get hit. It's one of our values, and it's why I'm alive today. When the first Marine came for me, I was lying on my face. He reached down and stuck his arms under my shoulders and lifted me off the ground. This was a very intimate ambush, a brawl really. And the machine gun was maybe nine, ten feet away. At that very moment, the NVA gunner fired a short burst into my chest that blew me out of the arms of the Marine who had just propped me up. I have no idea what happened to the first Marine, but presume he was killed. Then a second Marine came for me—an eighteen-year-old from Louisiana—and the NVA gunner shot him, too. It was the Marine's first firefight.

He fell to the ground next to me, holding his forearm. And I had this huge hole in my chest. It was big enough to stick a fist through. The rounds had blown away the top of my left lung and ripped through my ribs. At this point, I knew that I was dying. So I told him to leave me behind. I didn't want anyone else to die on my behalf. I remember him crying and firing his rifle back at the NVA with one hand and saying, "I'm not gonna leave you, Musky. I'm not gonna leave you!" And he didn't.

Jim Rye killed the NVA gunner. Jim was one of the bravest Marines I'd ever known. Though pursued by the North Vietnamese, he and another buddy, Dan Cooney, came for me and for our grenadier. They dragged us out by our wrists, even though they knew we were both dying. We'd both been shot through the chest, but somehow we were still alive.

Over the years, I've thought about the moments after I got shot, and in writing this book, I realized that I would have to tell this story as I've never told it before. I've come to understand that when people are badly hurt, they are, in effect, transported to a different place, someplace they've never been in their lives, and they are not fully aware of everything that's happening to them. So the challenge, in the days, weeks, and months after getting badly hurt, is to make a narrative out of your fragmented memories and perceptions of what took place and then make sense of what happened, put it back into a logical order, and learn how to tell the story. In order to figure out what happened to me when I was shot, I collected details from a horrible recurring dream that I had for about a year after it happened. In the dream, I would see the first Marine who tried to pick me up, lying a few yards away from me. I can still see him, as I did in the dream. The bullets had thrown us both a good distance and torn me from his hands. In the dream, his body is mangled and bleeding out. And each I time see him, I realize, once again, that I killed a Marine, which is far worse than being shot. When that Marine came up and grabbed me, the machine gunner shot us both.

It happened so fast that I couldn't tell what was going on. There was so much shooting, and I could hear a lot of screaming, so I knew I wasn't the only one hit. Jim and then some of my other buddies ran up and grabbed me by the flak jacket and started to drag me away. Then, because I was too heavy, they dropped me and started stripping off all my gear. I hated it. I lost my rifle. I had been carrying a whole bag of frags, and I loved my hand grenades. I always carried more than I had to, and I lost all those too. I hated the idea of the NVA getting all my gear and using it to kill more Marines. They tried to put a battle dressing on my chest, but the hole was too big. My flak jacket was open, and I looked down and saw the hole, and it was so big that my Saint Christopher, which I had strung on my dog-tag chain, disappeared inside it. And I thought, *Jesus Christ, that's a big hole.* So there were all these guys trying to help me, but the wound was too big and in an awkward spot, so they couldn't get the dressing tied on, and finally they just gave up trying. Four guys went to pick me up, but the battle was still raging, and I didn't understand why they were doing all this shit. So I said, "Leave me." I was so fucking thirsty; I'd never been thirstier. I started begging the guys for a drink of water, and one of them said, "We can't give you water," fearing that I might aspirate on it. And I said, "Yes, you can," and I'm talking with a blown-out chest, forming words between short gasps for air. "I'm dying," I told them. "Don't let me die thirsty." Against his better judgment, one of the guys gave me a drink of water, and it both kept me alive and made it easier for me to die. Worse than the pain of being shot through the chest was the anguish of being that thirsty.

Then they grabbed me by my arms and started dragging me along, and I realized they had fought their way out of the ambush, but there was still a fight going on, so they'd drop me and lie down on top of me and then pick me up and drag me some more. I was dying and they knew it, but they kept covering my body with theirs, as if I had a chance of making it out alive. "I'm done," I kept telling them, giving them permission to leave me and then getting scared that they might actually do it. Still, they never left me. They just kept picking me up and dragging me along. Finally, I grabbed Jim and I pulled him down to where my mouth was right next to his ear and I said, "Don't let them get me alive," because I didn't want my last moment on earth to be watching an NVA Soldier pull down my pants with a knife in his hand. My fear had gotten the best of me, and I put this horrible demand upon Jim because I knew he would do it. I trusted him and knew that if he had to do it, he would, even if he would never be able to forgive himself for it. Jim leaned over, looked me in the eye, and said, "Don't worry. They won't get you alive," and his words came as such a relief. The guys grabbed me again and dragged me again—I have no idea how many times—dropping me to fire back and then picking me up again.

When we made it back to the company, it was being hit. They pulled me into the casualty area, and all of a sudden Lieutenant Magee was there, and I'd never been so glad to see anybody. He pulled me up in his arms and was holding me and crying, which really blew me away. He was watching the remains of his old platoon being dragged in. The senior corpsman turned to him and said, "He's either shot through the heart or the lungs. There's nothing I can do for him." Then he walked away.

A helicopter came in, a CH-34, and they threw me into it. The corpsman inside stood over me, looked me up and down, saw that I was as good as dead, and then told the door gunner to get me "out of the way." They slid me under the feet of the port-side gunner. As we waited to take off, I saw holes begin to appear in the side of the helicopter. We were taking fire, but the crew held that bird on the ground until they had loaded up all the wounded.

On the flight to Delta Med at Dong Ha, the port-side gunner held my hand. Every time I started to fade, he squeezed it hard, pulling me back from death. If I had slipped away into unconsciousness, I would never have come back, and so when we landed, I was afraid to let go of his hand. He had to climb off the helicopter with me before he finally wrestled loose of my death grip. He was wearing a visor, and I wouldn't recognize him now if he walked up and punched me in the nose, but I'll never forget the way he looked at me before jumping back onto that CH-34 and taking off to collect more dying Marines.

They carried me into Delta Med and placed my stretcher on sawhorses. The place was strewn with wounded men. And I thought, *Okay, maybe there's a chance I'll make it. I've somehow made it this far.* I looked over at Blair, who was laid out beside me on my right, and I could see the bullet hole in the right side of his chest. He was unconscious, and that scared the shit out of me, because I believed he was dead. Then a doctor came over and inspected me. I was awake and alert. He methodically checked me over, taking in the gaping hole in my chest. He looked me square in the eyes and asked, "What's your religion, Marine?" "I'm a Protestant," I replied. And he shouted, "Get a chaplain over here! I can't help this man." That was when I thought, *This is really it—the end of the line.* There were so many wounded guys, screaming and struggling for life, and there was so much blood that it looked as if Delta Med had been painted red. They pulled my Saint Christopher out of the hole in my chest and told me that it had been resting against my heart. It was stained purple from soaking in my blood.

This chaplain came over and started to pray by my head. But then another surgeon—a redheaded doctor in a bloodstained T-shirt—walked by, and as he passed, I, having been raised in the Midwest always to be polite, smiled at him and nodded. The surgeon stopped, looked at me, and shouted, "Why isn't somebody helping this man?" And I thought, *Yeah, why isn't somebody helping this man?* The chaplain stepped aside, and the surgeon started working on me and giving orders. They still hadn't found my dog tags, because they were in my pocket, and so he said, "What's your blood type?" and when I told him, he shouted, "Get me blood right now!" and all of a sudden all kinds of guys were handling me again. Then he turned to me and said, "I'm sorry, Marine, but I'm going to have to hurt you." When you've got a chest wound, they can't give you morphine, because it would depress your respiratory system, so you have to take all the pain. But in my mind there was nothing that doctor could do that hadn't already been done.

He cut my side open and stuck something inside that separated my ribs. Then he shoved a tube right into my pleural cavity, to drain all the blood in which I'd been drowning. My breaths came a little easier then, in tight little gasps. I didn't think I had any screams left in me, but as it turned out, I had a last big one I'd been saving for that moment. It started down at the bottom of my feet and climbed all the way up and out my throat, until all the air had left my body. It was one of those horrible, sickening screams that you never want to hear, let alone coming from your own mouth. To this day, I don't know where I got the air to produce it.

A senior doctor at Delta Med came over and said, "We can't do anything for you here." And so they loaded me, along with Blair, onto a big four-engine C-130 and flew us to Alpha Med, a hospital in Phu Bai. We were miraculously still alive, and we were the only guys on that cavernous plane, except for a corpsman who kept changing out our blood bags. As quickly as he hung one, the blood flowed right out of us and he had to hang another. All the while I was praying for my family. All this time I was still conscious. I had to be. And without morphine, I just had to eat all the pain. When we landed at Alpha Med, four Marines ran in, grabbed my stretcher, and started carrying me down the ramp. I knew my buddy Pat Van Buren had been wounded at Con Thien and was down at Alpha Med, because he had written to me from there. So as the Marines were carrying my stretcher down the ramp, feetfirst, I lifted my head and said to one of them, "Van Buren." It was all I could find the breath to say. There were thousands of guys at Phu Bai, but to my amazement he immediately replied, "Patrick?" And I said, "Yeah, get him." And then he called another Marine over to help carry the stretcher, while he sprinted off to find Pat. Next thing I remember, one of my best friends in the world walked into receiving at Alpha Med, ran over to me, and grabbed my hand. It was Pat. "I'm here, Musky. I'm here." I knew I was dying, but it filled me with such joy to see him. I told him I was dying, and then they took me into X-ray and flopped me around so goddamn much I didn't know if I could take any more pain, but Pat stayed with me the whole time, holding my hand and reassuring me with his presence.

They wheeled me into surgery and told Pat that he had to get out. "You're going to have to throw me out of here," he said to them. "That's my buddy." And so they said, "Okay. Stay if you want, but put a mask on." One of the thoracic specialists, a lieutenant commander, led the surgery. As he put me to sleep, I thought, *Boy, this is really it. Okay, God. Into your hands I deliver my spirit.* I just gave my soul to Christ and I relaxed. I didn't have to fight anymore. I had done everything I could do, and I simply had nothing left to give, which came as a great relief. Finally, all of the pain, all of the fear, everything that had been terrifying me those past eleven and a half months, I could let it go. I believed I had died, that I was dead. So when I woke up in a Quonset hut, in a surgical intensive care ward, with a Catholic priest standing at the end of my bed reciting Latin, it got a bit surreal. Apparently, they had seen my Saint Christopher medal and presumed I was Catholic. As I listened to him administer what I assumed were last rites, I looked up at the priest and said, "Excuse me, Father, but I don't think I need that." To which he replied, "Well, of course you don't," flashing me a big-ass smile. I couldn't believe I was still alive. I wasn't out of the woods yet, but I was definitely looking at the woods. I later learned that they called the surgeon the "miracle worker." He certainly worked a miracle on me that day. His name was Lieutenant Commander Dr. Powell.

I ended up setting a record in the intensive care unit. They said usually a patient was either dead or transferred to another unit in three days. I was there at least seven, during which time they took me in and out of surgery. I looked over to my side and saw Blair and thought, *Oh, thank God he's still alive. I'm not alone.* I couldn't figure out why I was tied down, and Blair was too, but later I saw Blair have a seizure. And they told us that's why they had bound us. We were both having seizures. I'm glad that I never knew about it, because it scared the hell out of me watching Blair go through one. It was violent, and if they hadn't tied him down, he would have flown right out of that rack. They had placed my rack and Blair's next to the corpsman's desk. "We put the guys up here we like the most," they said, but later they told me they put the most serious cases right next to the desk so they could keep an eye on us. At night, there was a little light-bulb over each of our racks that looked like a half-moon. A few days later, a whole bunch of wounded guys were wheeled in, and I felt like an astronomer gazing at stars as I drifted in and out of consciousness.

One of the most memorable visits I received while recovering at Alpha Med was from General Bruno Hochmuth, who had been the commanding general of MCRD San Diego when I was a recruit there. He was now the commanding general of the Third Marine Division. He came over to my rack and to Blair's and decorated us. Blair told him that I'd been shot while trying to come for him, which was awfully nice of him. I still don't know how he knew that. Alongside General Hochmuth, there were Vietnamese generals and all kinds of other people, including a group of beautiful young women in traditional Vietnamese clothes called *áo dais,* tight-fitting long shirts worn over silk pants. They were stunningly gorgeous, and I thought to myself, *I'd rather be talking to them than to the generals.* But then General Hochmuth gave us Purple Hearts, and a Vietnamese general decorated us both with the Cross of Gallantry and with the Gold Star for Valor, which they told me was the highest order of this type of award. And I thought, *Even if I die, this will be nice for Mom and Dad.* They pinned the Cross of Gallantry on the pillow next to me and took a picture of me shaking the hand of

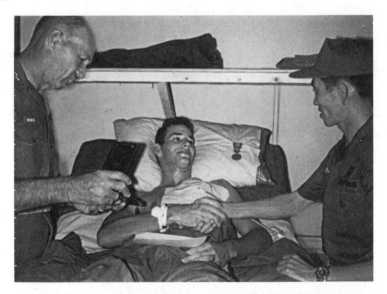

I receive the Purple Heart while recovering in a hospital bed at Third Medical Battalion, Phu Bai. Left to right, Gen. Bruno Hochmuth, CO Third Marine Division, Gen. Hoàng Xuân Lãm, CO Vietnamese Eleventh Division.

the Vietnamese general, who was the commanding general of I Corps.

As they were decorating us, I asked if I could recommend awards for the guys who had gotten me out, especially the ones I thought had been wounded or killed while attempting to save me. The general called over a major and said, "Get this guy's information." I pressed the major, and he turned to me and forcefully said, "I'm going to tell you something. You don't need to worry about that. Those two boys will get the Purple Heart. There is no medal that America gives that shows how much you love your country more than the Purple Heart. Besides, they were just doing their job." "Major, it was a lot more than that," I began to say, but I quickly lost steam. It was challenging to continue talking, given the state of my chest and lungs, and I was beginning to feel exhausted. Sweat was pouring off my skin, and I was counting the seconds until I could rest again. Then these schoolgirls from the city of Hue and a group of Vietnamese nurses came up to our beds and read a speech, thanking us for our sacrifices and for fighting for their freedom. They had made each of us a little white handkerchief with embroidery on it. I still have it. An especially beautiful Vietnamese nurse came over, took the little handkerchief, and started dabbing my forehead, soaking up my sweat and talking to me softly and gently in Vietnamese. I have no idea what she said, but it sounded wonderful, and I found the way she was speaking to me soothing and extremely comforting.

Two days later, General Hochmuth was killed, the only general ever to be killed in action in the history of the Marine Corps. Pat was on radio watch and heard the call come in. He quickly had somebody relieve him and came running down to the intensive care unit, leaned over my bed, grabbed my hand,

and whispered in my ear, low enough so that only I could hear, "General Hochmuth got killed." "Holy shit," I said. "How did that happen?" "They shot his helicopter down. I heard it come in over the radio." I had never shaken hands with a general before Hochmuth. They had to untie my right hand for the ceremony. When he talked with us, he didn't just read out citations, but spoke to each of us individually and made us feel special, as if he knew what he was doing. It was pretty heady stuff, almost impossible to process, that he was dead only two days after we shook hands.

When they separated us, Blair and I both cried. We'd been through a lot together, and I was happy that he was being transferred stateside to another hospital for treatment, but I didn't want to see him go. If it hadn't been for Pat, my spirits would have been completely crushed when they took Blair. In a situation like that, having a buddy with you makes all the difference in the world. The night after Blair left, they brought in another load of wounded, and they placed a kid across the aisle from me. He had also been hit at Con Thien and had multiple fragmentation wounds. When they brought him in, it was late, and I had been trying to sleep in fits and starts, between doses of morphine and waves of pain. The medical staff was down on the other end of the ward, working on somebody else, when the kid across from me seized. My legs were tied to the poles at the end of my bed, shoulder width apart, and all I could do was watch. He blew his tracheotomy tube out, and it landed in a spray of blood on the white sheet between my legs. I couldn't yell. I couldn't do anything to help him. I was completely helpless, and I thought to myself, *Oh my God. I don't want to witness another Marine dying.* He was seizing so badly that the medical staff heard him and came rushing down to his side, where they reinserted the trach and worked on him for a while. Sadly, he didn't make it, and I watched in horror as he died. In that low-light environment, it had a nightmarish quality to it.

Eventually, after many days in intensive care, I was wheeled into surgery so they could close up my chest. The hole was so big that they couldn't stretch the skin over it. One round had vaporized two of my ribs and a fist-size chunk of my pectorals and trapezius. Another round had lodged next to my spine, and they took that one out through my back. The surgeon had to use wire to suture the holes, but I could still look inside the cavity, because they weren't able to force the skin to come together. I had wire in my chest in two places, because they had put another chest tube in—one up top and one down below. I also had wire sutures in my side and down my back, right between my shoulder blades. If the bullet had entered one-half inch to the left, it would have severed my spine. After they wired me up, they loaded me onto a medevac and flew me up to Da Nang, where I recovered for a few days, before they flew me to Tachikawa, Japan, where I went straight into the surgery ward again, because my condition was still pretty questionable. Then they put me on a plane.

On the flight, I had a nurse assigned to me who was also assigned to another kid in my section. We were both fucked up, but he was in far worse shape than I. He had shrapnel lodged in his heart but somehow was still alive. There had been a lot of news stories written about this poor kid who had been hit at Con Thien and was on his way home to see his parents and his girl, who were waiting for him at Scott Air Force Base in St. Louis. On the way, we stopped at a hospital in the Philippines. They wheeled us off the plane and into receiving, where we were greeted by a bunch of American girls. They were dependents, children of military families stationed there, and I was told they were on a tour of the hospital. At this point, I still had Con Thien mud all over me, and I couldn't remember when I had last washed my hair or when I had last shaved. And now, for the first time in damn near a year, I was looking at American girls, and they were looking back at us, horrified. It was only a quick exchange, because we were immediately wheeled off to X-ray and then the surgery ward, but I'll never forget it.

Next we were flown to Alaska, and then on to Scott Air Force Base, just outside St. Louis. We were flown there because it was the closest airstrip to the Great Lakes Naval Hospital. When we landed, they wheeled the other Marine off the plane and put a curtain stand around his stretcher. We were all on the same ward. The only privacy they could give him was the curtain. His family was waiting for him there. His girlfriend walked up and went behind the curtain, and as soon as he saw her, he died. He had held on all that way, with shrapnel in his heart, only to die when he arrived home. He just wanted to see his girl one last time.

I spent the night at Scott Air Force Base, where the Red Cross had set up a phone bank, from which I was allowed to call home. They told me I had only three minutes to talk, but I remember the Red Cross lady coming up to me and saying, "Don't worry about it. Talk as long as you want." So I got to talk to Mom, and it meant the world to me to hear her voice. The next day, they flew me to the Great Lakes Naval Hospital in Chicago, which was an approximately thirty-minute flight from St. Louis. When we landed, it was late at night. The airstrip was pitch-black, and they quickly moved me through receiving and X-ray and took me up to the surgery ward. On the way, I passed dozens of guys in the hallways on gurneys, but I was lucky enough to get a rack on the surgery ward.

While he was performing my exam, I asked the medical officer, "Why'd you bring us in so late, Doc?" There had been something awkward and strange about being wheeled into this huge hospital—naked under a sheet—after midnight. We'd all been raised on films in which the wounded came home from World War II and Korea and were met by marching bands and cheering crowds, welcoming them home. By contrast, it felt as if we were being snuck in under the cover of night, as if they didn't want us to be seen. "It's for your protection," the medical officer replied. "What?" I said. "I don't need protection. I'm home." And he said, "We had people gathering out here, throwing things and screaming obscenities and insults as they unloaded the wounded from the planes. So they just started bringing you guys in late at night." It took a little while for the reality of what he was telling me to sink in. When I left for Vietnam, the peace movement hadn't really taken off. They weren't holding giant marches yet. That all started in 1967. On the deceptively short

Me (right) and Dan Cooney. My oldest son was named after him.
We flew home from the hospital to surprise Mom for Mother's Day.

voyage home, all I could think about was how lucky I was to be returning to the safety and comfort of Independence, Missouri, to the warm embrace of my family and friends, and the support of neighbors and teachers and citizens who had beamed with pride when I deployed. But as I mulled over the word "protection," it slowly dawned on me that the America I had left behind when I shipped out for Vietnam was not the America to which I had returned. The country had changed. Though I had been away for less than a year, it seemed as if I had arrived in another decade, and I never felt as though I were home—really home—ever again.

Me and Sharon "Missy" Van Buren in bathing suits after I returned from Vietnam; you can see the scar on my chest.

BOOK THREE
———

MARCHING AGAINST THE WAR

CHAPTER 11

Leaving the Corps

Aﬆer returning to the states and completing my basic recovery, I got assigned to Weapons Training Battalion at Marine Corps Base Quantico, Virginia, which is about forty minutes south of Washington, D.C. It was there in the D.C. area that I first experienced how much American attitudes had changed toward service personnel since I left for Vietnam. Even when out of uniform, in my civvies, it was pretty obvious from my high and tight haircut, the way that I walked—with shoulders squared and head erect—and my injured left arm that I was military, and I did have a few people spit on the sidewalk in front of me when they saw me coming and others who just gave me dirty looks. I never got assaulted or spat on, though. That happened to other guys, and I'm not sure I could have handled it if it had happened to me. I would probably have come unglued. On occasion, people did drive by and shout, "Baby killer!" out of car windows, but never to my face. Sometimes, I'd walk into a restaurant with a group of Marines, and the host or hostess would refuse to serve us. They wouldn't even seat us and would just let us stand there until we figured it out.

The worst experience that I remember from that time occurred one spring afternoon when I was walking around D.C., taking in the sights, wearing my uniform, truly proud to be a Marine. I strolled up to an intersection, the lights changed, and this beautiful young woman walked up next to me and asked me if I had been wounded in Vietnam. "Well, yes, ma'am," I said, thinking how great it was that this pretty girl was talking to me and hoping the conversation could develop into something more. But as soon as she heard my answer, her face twisted into this hateful scowl as if a mask had slipped off, revealing her true face. "You should have been killed over there," she said. I was so shocked by her words that I didn't even have a comeback. I just stood there, dumbstruck, as the light changed and she crossed the street. Suddenly I had an overwhelming feeling of missing Vietnam. I wanted to go back. I know it's contradictory to say, but as senseless as much of my war experience had been, the war was the only place where everything made sense. Combat had become my normal. Civilian life couldn't have felt more foreign.

I was only nineteen when I was living in Virginia, and I didn't know many people in the area. My relationship with Karen had not survived the length of our separation. We were kids, and the duration had just been too long. My cousin was stationed in Norfolk, and I went down to visit him from time to time. We'd pull out our IDs at bars and tell people we were brothers, and they'd buy us lots of free drinks because they couldn't believe a Marine and a Sailor could get along, and that felt good, but Norfolk was a military town. We'd all been told that the girl-to-guy ratio in D.C. was five to one, and I was excited by those odds. One day, out of the blue, I got a call from a girl named Shirley who had come with a group of other young women from Kan-

Me and my cousin Richard Musgrave home from the war, 1969.

sas City to D.C. to attend airline school. She had heard about
me from some of my old high school buddies whom she and
her friends had dated back home. They had told her, "When
you get out there, give John a call. He's a good guy." And so we
started dating.

A corporal on my range, Michael Medcoff, who I believe was
from West Virginia, drove a beautiful white Mustang convertible. He and I became friends, and his fiancée, who was a terrific
person, and the girl I had been dating lived in D.C. apartments
that were just blocks away from each other. So Michael and I
would regularly drive up in his hot rod and take our ladies out
on the town. On the night that Dr. King was murdered, April 4,
1968, we were planning one such evening, but D.C. descended
into violence and unrest. Martial law was declared, and the city
ignited in flames.

It was a surreal experience, driving through D.C. to pick
up our girls and not being able to see the Capitol through
the smoke. It looked as if we were at war and felt like it, too.

While we were over in Vietnam, there was a riot in Detroit, and a picture of whole neighborhoods ablaze had run on the front page of the Pacific edition of *The Stars and Stripes,* which was the only source of news we had over there. They would send the newspapers out to us in sandbags if there was room with the other supplies, whenever we were getting resupplied in the bush. Supposedly, it was to boost our morale. But there was a photo of tanks and troops from the Eighty-Second Airborne moving through the streets of Detroit, and our reaction was, "Holy shit! That's the Eighty-Second Airborne. Why the fuck aren't they over here now?" One of my fellow Marines, who came from Detroit, looked up and said, "What the fuck are they doing in my neighborhood? And what the fuck am I doing here if there's a war in my neighborhood?" At first I thought he was bullshitting, but he seemed legitimately shaken. Eight thousand miles away, surrounded by people we didn't know and who didn't want us there, he saw a photo of his own neighborhood in flames with tanks driving down the goddamn street. No wonder he was rattled. While we were at war, the country went to war with itself, and when we came home, that war was just getting started.

Things with Shirley eventually petered out, and I began learning the hard way that the dating field for active-duty Marines was actually pretty slim. The local girls were mostly off-limits, because their families wouldn't let them date Marines, primarily for two reasons: one, most of the fathers were World War II vets who saw us as horny, out-of-control gorillas; and, two, the negative attitudes about Vietnam veterans had begun to bleed over into the civilian world from the peace movement. While stationed in Quantico, Virginia, I actually went out with a female Marine, of which I had met only two during my whole time in the Corps. One of them worked at the snack bar at the shooting range, and when her friend, a female lance corporal who was the receptionist to the undersecretary of the Navy, came to visit, I mustered all of my courage and asked her out. Nothing really came of it, but it was refreshing dating her, because it required less energy to talk with her than with other women. She spoke the same language I did, and we didn't need an interpreter to carry on a conversation. Now, when I see all of the women in the armed forces, I sort of envy people serving today, because they have people around them who understand their motivations and what they are dealing with, which sure would have helped me in those days on many an awkward date.

During my time at Quantico, I was recovering from not only physical wounds but emotional ones, too, though I didn't understand it at the time. I was drinking pretty heavily, trying to numb all of the pain. Over the summer, Marine Reserve units would come to Quantico for two-week stints, and we had to run them through requalification on the range, just like active-duty Marines; the reserve units had to requalify every year. And so I got to meet a lot of older guys in reserve units who had served in previous conflicts. They were legends in my book. These were the guys who inspired me to want to be a Marine. They could have been at Iwo Jima or Guadalcanal. After sessions on the range, many of them headed straight for the snack bar, where they would start drinking, and because they had been told that I had been shot up in Vietnam, they treated me with a great deal of respect, buying me all the beer that I could swallow and having fun watching me get drunk.

There was one time in particular, after having a few drinks with the guys after work, when I had my first flashback. All I remember is that while stumbling out of the snack bar and saying my goodbyes one Saturday night, I caught my finger in the screen door and it really hurt. Next thing I knew I was waking up in the base hospital on Sunday morning. One of my bud-dies who had been with me the night before told me that when I banged my finger, I stopped, looked down at it, and, when I saw blood pouring out of it, looked up and said, "Oh my God! I'm hit!" and down I went. Apparently, I fell to the ground as if I had been shot and relived the entire experience of being blasted through the chest at Con Thien, gasping for breath, say-ing my prayers, and believing I was on the verge of death. Some-how they got me through the whole ordeal and then called for an ambulance to come get me. When the ambulance arrived, I freaked out and started reliving the ambush all over again. At the hospital, they gave me something, I'm not sure what, that knocked me out cold, and when I came to the next day, I felt like absolute shit. I didn't have my boots, because they took them off before loading me into the ambulance. Dicky, my Sailor cousin, who had been visiting me at the base, stayed there with me, by my rack in the hospital, the entire night, and tried to keep me from getting written up, telling the medical officer, "Doc, just let me have him. I've gotten him through this before." He knew I wanted to stay in the Corps and managed to persuade the hospital to cut me loose with just a stern word about not drinking so much, but nothing about my having a flashback. As we were leaving, I got the impression that it was a pretty common thing for them to see in those days.

I caught a ride back up to the range, and when I got there, I received word that the sergeant major wanted to see me. *Oh, fuck. Sergeant Major's on base on a Sunday. My ass is fucking finished,* I thought. Then I was told, "He wants to see you right the fuck now!" So I ran back to my room and threw on my boots and my special utilities, which had been pressed so I didn't look like ten pounds of shit in a five-pound bag. When I got over to see him, I stepped up and reported in, and he asked me if I'd had a good weekend. And I said, "Well, you know, Sergeant Major, it didn't work out too good." For some reason, the sergeant major liked me, and I sure liked him and looked up to him. Whenever he'd see me, I always had my uniform squared away and always had a good, positive attitude. It turned out he was just concerned and wanted me to be careful. He asked me if I was in trouble. "No, no," I said. "Marines drink. It's what we're made to do." And he said, "We're just concerned because it didn't work out very good for you last night, did it?" And I said, "No, sir, it didn't." "Well, then maybe you ought to find a better way of doing things," he suggested. "They were buying me beers, Sergeant Major," I said. "I couldn't not drink them. I didn't want to be a snob." He got a chuckle out of that and sent me on my way, and I felt as though I'd really dodged a bullet that time.

Seeing how serious I was about being a Marine, the guys at the hospital started calling me "junior lifer" and even referred to me by the nickname Gunny Musgrave. At first it was supposed to be a dig. I was never gunnery sergeant material, but the name stuck because I had a "two-year lifer" attitude and was absolutely convinced that I wasn't going to become disabled. When they told me that the injuries I had sustained in combat were permanent, I thought, *Bullshit.* I just wasn't hearing it. I had accepted I could be killed. I even expected it. But then when I wasn't killed, it took me years to process what it meant to survive.

When I got back, at first I couldn't make sense of the fact that my left arm was a problem, because I hadn't been hit in the arm. When the bullets struck my chest, they instantly destroyed so much muscle, tissue, and bone that they left a huge wound. The doctors had stretched everything as close together as they could, but the hole hadn't fully closed. In the summer of 1968, I hadn't gotten it through my head that in order to fully close, the scars themselves needed to stretch, and as they stretched, the process gradually began to limit the mobility of my left arm and hand. As this was happening, I remained in complete denial. I figured it was horseshit. I would overcome it, and it just required some mind over fucking matter. They started me on a physical therapy regimen, and I fully committed myself to the task, PT every day for twelve months, believing I could beat this son of a bitch. I had a goal. Every morning, I'd work on the range, and in the afternoon I'd go to the PT room in the basement of the hospital, and my physical therapist would put me through the paces. In late 1968, I was promoted to the rank of corporal. Though I very much wanted to attend the promotion ceremony, I had to miss it because I was in the hospital doing physical therapy when it took place. One of the sergeants that I worked closely with on the range got my warrant, the certificate of my promotion, and brought it to me later that day. It was a huge moment for me, and I took my dress blue trousers straight to the tailor to have the blood stripe added down the seam, signifying that I was finally a noncommissioned officer, or NCO. By 1969, in spite of my promotion and all of the hard work I had put into my recovery it began dawning on me that things weren't going to change, but I had a really difficult time accepting it.

The main thing I couldn't swallow was this word that, growing up, I had always heard used about kids who had polio. My brother and I had been exposed to the disease, and there was a big scare about whether we might end up paralyzed or in an iron lung. The leg braces worn by polio survivors came to symbolize the word, which I couldn't allow myself to think or say. The kids were "crippled," which at the time had this really strong connotation. If you were crippled, you weren't a fully functioning human being. Young man or old, it didn't matter. That's what

I had internalized from my youth, and it proved so toxic that I did everything I could to rebel against it. Mainly, this meant I was drinking more and more, which allowed me to remain in denial about the permanence of some of my injuries.

All this time, I was still cultivating the fantasy that I would get stronger, regain full mobility, someday redeploy to Vietnam. But no matter how much I drank, reality kept catching up with me. I still had to keep going to Med boards, where a group of officers would look at my charts, ask me questions, assess my recovery, and determine if I could stay in and finish my enlistment. Over time, the evaluations kept getting harder, in large part because my recovery had stalled and I didn't seem to be making much progress. First I had a Med board at Quantico. Then they sent me to do one in Bethesda. Then I had to do an even bigger one at Henderson Hall, the headquarters of the Marine Corps, at which a final decision was to be made regarding my fate. I had hope right until the day of the evaluation. I figured they'd let me stay in the Corps because they'd see how committed I was to staying in and beating this thing. I just needed a little more time. By that point, in the spring of 1969, I had been back for more than a year, and things weren't improving. I was really just grasping at straws.

My mom and dad were always telling me about how I needed to make plans outside the Marine Corps. So I went to the PX and found a book on how to prepare for college entrance exams. I took it with me back to the range and then to the barracks and spent a couple of weekends poring over its pages. I didn't know half of the answers to the sample questions, and it made me feel like a total cretin. In high school, I did what I had to do to get decent enough grades so Dad wouldn't lock me in the basement and would allow me to enlist, but I never took seriously the idea of applying to college. When Jay and I got out of there, we were on the road to adventure. We left Independence and Sugar Creek, Missouri, in our dust; Van Horn High School could go fuck itself. School had not been a positive experience for me, and leaving it felt like escaping from prison. So after I picked up that book and saw how little I knew, I thought, *This ain't going to work. There's no way I'm going to college if I have to pass this fucking test before they'll let me in. It's impossible.* I told Dad that maybe I could work at General Motors. By that time he had ascended to upper management at the plant in Fairfax, Kansas, which was the second-largest automobile manufacturing plant in the country. I knew Dad could get me a job because he got Butch one there during the summer, and he'd arranged for other people's sons to work there, too. While the thought of working in a factory was enough to make me want to blow my head off, I had to have something to say for myself, some kind of plan B, if things didn't work out with the Marine Corps. Still, I held out hope right up to the final Med board.

On every base, an NCO was tasked with the responsibility of getting Marines to reenlist. There were signs all over the place, reading, "Sgt. Sam says, 'It's a great career,'" and things to that effect. Well, I used to stop the reenlistment sergeant out on the grinder, because he'd always be buttonholing the other guys about reenlisting but never me. I'd say, "Look, Sergeant. I will reenlist right now if you'll give me door gunner school orders to go back to Vietnam," because it was clear to me by then that I couldn't be a grunt anymore, but I still thought I could be a helicopter door gunner. Once I got to Vietnam, I knew they wouldn't send me back, so I figured I just had to get there and then I'd be able to survive. I could still do the job, and everything would be copacetic. Well, of course, everything wasn't copacetic and I knew it, but I thought I was tossing him a pretty good deal. And he kept saying, "Look, you've got to be able to pass the reenlistment physical, and I don't think you will." And I said, "You wait until this last Med, and I'm going to get this shit squared away, and then we'll talk, okay?"

In those days you could bring a lawyer to represent you in the Med board, and a young lieutenant just out of law school was assigned as my counsel. He looked over my papers and told me that he felt confident I could get 100 percent from the board. We went in to face the board, and they started asking me questions. The lieutenant tried to get me to read from a script and to let him do all the talking. But I told him, "No, sir. I'm good to go." They went over my physical therapy results and reviewed my medical records. They had me attempt to do certain things to prove that I had full use of my left arm. Then they asked questions about what I would do if I got medically retired. By that point, though, their minds were already made up. I was still convinced there was a way forward and was playing for more time to get well before they put me out the door. And that's when they tossed me out of the Marine Corps into the civilian world, like a goldfish into a swimming pool full of piranhas. At the end of the report, they rated me 70 percent. The lieutenant was pissed and said, "If you would have just kept your mouth shut, I could have gotten you at least ninety." I asked him if there was a way to appeal the decision, and he said, "No. There's just your retirement board. That's the last shot you've got." I couldn't hear what he was saying. My mind wasn't able to grasp it. I still thought maybe I could appeal the decision and possibly get a few more months. As far as I was concerned, this was the firing squad. For about a year or so after I left the Corps, whenever people asked me about what had happened, I'd say, "They shitcanned me," because that's how it felt, as if I were a piece of broken equipment that had been tossed in the junk heap.

CHAPTER 12

Big Vet on Campus

I was twenty years old, and I didn't have the Corps anymore. I didn't have my buddies anymore. I was no longer a professional. I was a cripple in the deep end of the cesspool. I was in a hostile environment for which I was not equipped, physically or emotionally. There was no turning back. People kept talking to me about my plans for the future, but I didn't know what that word meant anymore. I had discarded it in the bush. If I had money, I spent it. I was totally impatient and full of aggression. To deal with it all, I kept on doing what I had been doing for the past couple of years. I drank. I pissed away my life. I did stupid things. People who knew me would ask, "Why are you doing this shit?" And I'd say, "The world is going to end at midnight, motherfucker." It was the world that I lived in, and I couldn't figure out what to do. I spent an entire summer drinking, and the only job that I held down was as a counselor at a church camp I'd attended as a kid. I didn't drink on the job, because I still felt an obligation to set an example for my kids. I saw myself as their squad leader, and they won every award that summer, because I motivated their asses. They called themselves Gunny's Gorillas. I did what I knew how to do. I led.

By that point, I was already suicidal, and everything I fucked up made me feel as if I didn't deserve to live and that I was unworthy of the sacrifices my friends had made. It was classic survivor's guilt, but I didn't even know what that was yet. I hadn't paid any attention to what I'd been told about transitioning back to civilian life, and I had no idea that as a veteran I would receive benefits from the VA, including college tuition, until someone from the VA contacted me and asked me to come in to talk. I went and he told me that I would get to go to college. I didn't believe him at first, but he explained that because I was disabled, the VA had a special financial opportunity for me, as well as programs to help me prepare for college. So, at his suggestion, I went to visit the University of Missouri–Kansas City, because I had buddies from high school who went there, and I also visited the University of Kansas, which was the biggest school within an hour of home. But as I walked the campuses of those enormous state schools, I was simply overwhelmed by the crowds—thousands of people—and I knew I wouldn't be able to make it in that environment. It was also obvious that I was a disabled vet, and I caught a lot of negative reactions.

Karen, the girl I had been in love with when I left for the Corps, had gone to a small, private liberal arts school, Baker University, about an hour away in Baldwin City, Kansas. She had ended up transferring to the University of Missouri, but every time I saw her mother at church on Sunday, she'd say, "You really ought to go check out Baker." I told her I would, and never really got around to it, but she kept after me until finally I said, "If I go down there and look at the place, will that be enough for you?" And she said, "That's all I want you to do." At her prompting, I called up Baker, made an appointment, got out my map, and drove to Baldwin City to check out the campus. When I pulled off the state highway in my MGB with the top down, I sped down this little road lined with giant trees, so overgrown that their branches met in the middle and formed a junglelike canopy. As I approached the edge of town, the streets widened and turned from asphalt to brick. Suddenly I found myself in a beautiful place that seemed uncannily familiar—a small, quiet, peaceful midwestern town. It was a little bigger than Paradise, where I had spent my early childhood years, but not by much. In the center of town stood a small business district—so small that it had not a square but an L—and a pretty little campus, full of open lawns, shaded by ancient trees, and ringed with old stone buildings.

The first guy I talked to was a Vietnam veteran named Ken Snow who was the head of admissions and in his early thirties. His wife was also a vet, an Army nurse, and they had gone to the war together after they got married. So I felt right at home with these people, and they rolled out the red carpet for me. Baker was the second most expensive school in the state, a private university affiliated with the Methodist Church, and they told me that because it was a small school, I would never be just a number there. I'd be an individual. If I was struggling in a class, I could talk to the professor, because the faculty all lived in the neighborhood and they'd be able to help. They also told me there were a number of other student-veterans on campus and that they really believed I could succeed there. So I thought, *Maybe this will work. I've got nothing to lose. Because of my VA benefits, called vocational rehabilitation, I'm going to get paid to go.* By then, I was collecting 100 percent disability from the VA, which was a fairly good check in those days, roughly four hundred dollars a month, which in 1969 was serious money. Plus I'd receive a stipend as a student, and I'd have a charge account at the bookstore. I wouldn't have to pay for anything. *What the hell?* I thought. On the campus tour, I had seen a whole lot of pretty girls and entertained the idea that maybe they wouldn't all have the attitude I had encountered on the East Coast. Nobody was giving me any shit. In fact, it seemed like a welcoming place. This was just a few weeks before the freshman year would start, and I told Ken that I didn't have time to take the entrance exams. He reassured me, saying, "Don't worry about it. If you want to go here, I'll get you in. You come here in three weeks for orientation, and I'll have you enrolled." And I told him, "I won't have any money that soon." "Don't worry about it," he said. "We'll take you on faith. We know the VA is going to cover it. So just come down."

This was the first thing that looked good to me since I'd come home. I was speaking to a Vietnam vet who told me there were other vets on campus and that it wouldn't be like at those big universities, where people would invariably be giving me shit. And they didn't care if I was academically unprepared. They would work with what I gave them, if I came to the table with a good attitude. I put on my Marine Corps thinking cap and said to myself, "If I'm going to make this work, then I need to be motivated," and I took on going to Baker as a mission. Three weeks later, I showed up with my MGB packed to the gills and entered as a freshman. All of the first-year students had to live in a dorm, which, naturally, I tried to get out of, but they held firm. In the end, they did allow me to keep my MGB on cam-

pus, which made a big difference and gave me an escape hatch,
if I needed it.

Next thing I knew I was a freshman at Baker. Before I really
got my head wrapped around what that meant, I was going to
class and, of course, drinking like a fish at night. No matter
what, though, I always got up the next morning and dragged
myself to class, because my professors were all truly looking out
for me, going out of their way to say, "If you have any trouble,
call me at home," or inviting me over to dinner. That's how I
made my way, through the kindness of those professors, who
were all rooting for me. One of my requirements that year
was biology. I hadn't taken it in high school, and I had no idea
what to expect. I walked into the lab and was greeted by a little
white-haired man who happened to be a highly respected and
internationally known biologist named Dr. Ivan Boyd.

Before coming to class, I had to go to the bookstore and pick
up a lab kit, and when I opened the kit, I saw that there were
scalpels in it. On the first day of class, Dr. Boyd announced that
we would be dissecting animals, and I put the fucking brakes on
right at the door. I said, "I ain't cutting nothing open that looks
like a human being inside." I told him, "Doc, I cannot do this."
I knew that if they opened up one of these things in front of me,
I was going to run screaming out of the room. I said I couldn't
do it, and Dr. Boyd was fine. He knew I wasn't going to be a
biology major and that I just needed to get through his class. So
he said I could be a lab assistant and hand out worksheets and
other materials, and I wouldn't ever have to cut anything open.

One of the nicest things about Baker was that the courses
were all pass-fail. If you worked really hard and pursued extra
credit, you could earn a high pass, and I was so determined
that I got all high passes my freshman year. When I learned

*I wouldn't sit for a yearbook photo at Baker, so they took this
in the student union with my girlfriend and put it in the yearbook, 1969.*

about my grades, I walked right over to the dean's office and
asked him to send a letter to Marine Corps Headquarters, telling them that Corporal John D. Musgrave had achieved over
and above the requirements of his classes. I wanted the Marine
Corps to know that I was kicking ass, but I still held out hope
they might let me back in someday. When you first retired, it
was temporary. In five years, they would call you back, take a
look at you, and determine if you were permanently retired.
I made Dean Malicky write that letter because the only way I
could stay motivated was if I believed the Corps would see how
well I was doing and say, "Hey, we need him back." It was wish-
ful thinking, of course, but necessary for my survival.

I had to pick a major at the end of my freshman year. I didn't
know shit about majors. I thought, *I'm a corporal. How can
I "acquire" a major?* At Con Thien, Leonard Blair and I would
sometimes talk about what he had studied in college, and I'd
ask him dumb questions like "How does politics have a science?

I've only heard of biology and earth science." So he explained what political science was as if he were talking to a fifth grader. "It's the study of political systems and how politics work in society," he said. "Okay. Well, what about sociology? What the fuck is that?" I'd ask. "Sociology is the study of societies," he'd say, and then proceed to tell me about the types of things people learn in sociology classes. So when it came time for me to declare a major, I chose to double major in sociology and political science, because the only subject areas I knew about were the ones Leonard Blair had described to me in a foxhole in Con Thien, answering all of my stupid questions with the patience of a saint. Blair unknowingly put me on track for my college education. I owe it all to him.

In the beginning of my time at Baker, I wore what I called my Class A Civilian Attire to class, which featured slacks, short-sleeve collared shirts, and wing tips. One day, a few veterans invited me to meet them in the student union for some pointers on how to get by as a veteran on campus. I figured I could use some pointers, so I took them up on their offer. A few of the guys were Army, a few Navy, one was National Guard, and a couple of them were Vietnam vets. They sat me down and told me to pledge a fraternity, to never wear anything that reflected the military (even my current attire, which was too squared away to pass), to let my hair grow long, and to never under any circumstances talk about the military.

The longer I listened to them, the tighter I clenched my jaw, until finally I couldn't take any more talk of assimilation and burst up out of my chair, "Thank you. But no thank you. No fucking thank you!" I took my little attitude, walked outside, jumped into my MGB, and drove all the way back to Sugar Creek. When I got home, I went straight down to the basement, opened my seabags, pulled out my jungle jacket and my jungle boots, and raced over to the barbershop and got me a high and tight. I wasn't about to back down from what I was, which was a Marine. *You guys may be college students,* I thought, *but I am in God's own United States Marine Corps. And I will be fucked if I'm going to act like I'm embarrassed about it.*

Suddenly I had a new mission, which was to show everybody on that fucking campus that I wasn't the least bit impressed by their bullshit and I had no desire to blend in with them. Most of the people on campus were pretty careful around me, but after a number of negative encounters in the D.C. area and on other college campuses in which civilians had unloaded all of their negative feelings about the war on me, as if I were a symbol of the war itself, I was extra sensitive to any comment or attitude that seemed to imply that I had something to be ashamed of because of my military service. In those days, I wasn't walking around with a chip on my shoulder; there was a goddamn tree on my shoulder, which grew heavier each time I came into contact with the antiwar movement on campus, especially because I was the only vet there who approached things this way. Baker was a small campus, around a thousand students, but I was meeting lots of guys my age who had been undergraduates for five years or more. This was an expensive school, so these were people of privilege, and the only thing they were worried about was holding on to their class II-S draft permit student deferments. So when I got into conversations with them, I didn't even pretend to respect them. I'd ask, "You know what the II stands for in the II-S draft permit? Too scared." I was kind of an asshole about it in those days. *I may have to swim in the same water as these guys,* I thought, *but I ain't one of them.*

On October 15, 1969, we had our first Moratorium to End

the War in Vietnam, a huge national demonstration and teach-in, during which everything shut down as campuses all across the country protested the war. So I put on what I like to call my Fuck-You Jacket, with my company's insignia and nickname—the Walking Dead—emblazoned across the back, and I went down to Rice Auditorium, where everyone had gathered because it was raining. Outside, a small group of students was walking around, carrying American flags and holding up signs that said, "I support the troops in Vietnam." Somebody walked up and asked me if I wanted a flag, and I said, "Fucking A right! I'll take one," and extended my hand. I started walking around with these guys, some of whom I'd already met, because they had brothers in Vietnam and I knew they supported the military. By this time, Nixon had already announced that the war was a draw, which to me meant surrender. I had come to despise that son of a bitch, because he was still sending kids over there to die. During the election, he had assured Americans of a secret plan he had that would save lives, which he wouldn't disclose until he was elected president. It turned out that his secret plan was to withdraw troops but to keep sending poor kids overseas to fight the war. He didn't give a shit about us, and more working-class kids and kids of color continued to die. More than twenty thousand died in his so-called withdrawal, despite his so-called Vietnamization strategy. Needless to say, I wasn't thrilled about the direction of the war. My personal feeling at that point was that we should either get in all the way or get out. But I would be goddamned if I was going to protest with those people. They were the type who called me "war criminal," which happened a few times on campus, and turned their backs on me. *There ain't no fucking way I'm going to walk around with them,* I thought.

The campus was pretty small, as I said, so everybody knew everybody. A group of these kids, who knew me from class or other school functions, saw me walking around with the flag and came over to talk with me and asked if I'd like to address them inside the auditorium. I thought to myself, *Yeah, I ain't scared of you,* and I carried my flag up to the stage with no idea of what I was going to say but a desire to say something. To this day, I have no idea what they expected, but I knew I wasn't going to give them a speech about the war.

"Look, I've got buddies over there right now, and what you're doing right now, they think you're doing it against them," I said. "I want you to know that we think we're fighting for your right to say no, and we don't understand why you hate us. We don't understand why you are waving the flag of the guys who are killing us. And if you don't hate us, well, then I've got some names and addresses right here on me that I will give to you right now so you can write to my buddies and tell them why you're against this war and reassure them that you're not against them. Because we think we're dying for you, and you're treating us like shit. It's our fight, but it ain't our war. We didn't start it. And I think most of my buddies would probably agree with you. So what I'm asking you is this. If you're going to be pissed off at somebody, don't be pissed off at us. We don't have shit to do with it. We're just dying over there. If you want to end the war, be pissed off at the people that started it. That's all those assholes in Washington, D.C. It ain't all those kids you went to high school with who wouldn't turn and run away from their country."

The crowd of student protesters stood up and gave me a standing ovation. It blew me away and, for a fleeting moment, softened my pissed-off-ed-ness about the antiwar movement.

I walked back outside and rejoined the group carrying flags in support of the troops overseas, but soon found myself surrounded, not by students, but by professors who wanted to address what I had said inside. One pompous philosophy professor started hammering on me right away, saying how he was going to prove to me the fallacy of my beliefs while adamantly claiming that we were fighting the peace-loving Vietnamese, to which I said, "That's bullshit, buddy." We started to get into it. I told him we had killed communist Chinese over there, which he said was a lie. "I've seen their bodies," I said, but he insisted that all we had killed were innocent Vietnamese people who didn't want war. This wasn't going so well, and I was starting to get pretty angry, when he hit me with the perfect professor argument, to show what an idiot I was. "How many books have you read?" he asked. I was stunned. I just couldn't believe he said it. "Well, Doc, how many wars have you fought in?" I replied, glaring at him. He told me that was irrelevant. "It's not nearly as irrelevant as your question about books, buddy. We're talking about war, not a classroom discussion," I said as I pushed past him. I knew if I continued talking with him, it was going to get ugly, and that wouldn't have gone well for me, given the power dynamic. So I walked away.

From that point on I became a somewhat controversial figure on the small Baker campus. Some students thought I was cool for what I said, and others didn't. The general feeling was that my words had made sense, and most people agreed with the sentiment of what I said, even if they disagreed with my position on the war. To my surprise, some of the protesters invited me to a planning meeting, which I thought was weird, but I went just the same. I wanted to show them I was willing to engage with them, that what I said wasn't just hot air. They asked me some pretty good questions about the best way to phrase their letters to troops overseas. "Don't make them feel like Nazis," I said. "And if you really want to do something, send a package." I told them how the infantry units needed every-thing from socks to fruit cocktails. "I'll give you a list with addresses. I'll write up a list of things that would make them feel good." Sending them care packages would go a long way toward starting a dialogue, I suggested. "If you want them to consider your position, you'd better try to communicate with them, not win an argument." One woman said to me, "I think you all are a bunch of fascists." And I said, as respectfully as I could, "Well, I would suggest you not put that in your letters, because the guys over there wouldn't get beyond the first para-graph before wiping their asses with it."

As I was leaving the meeting, one of the students, a guy named Bill Richardson, asked me if I wanted to grab a beer. He was from a well-to-do family from Jacksonville, Florida, and he turned out to be one of the most extraordinary men I've ever met. He said, "I've been thinking about going into the service to fly helicopters." I thought, *The war sucks, but I'd be interested in talking with you about that,* and said, "Sure, if you're buying. You bet." So Bill and I went out drinking that night and became fast friends. Within minutes of sitting down with him at the bar, I knew he was okay, and I also somehow knew that I could trust him and even count on him. We were from totally differ-ent worlds but were cut from the same cloth. His dad had been a B-26 Pilot in the Army Air Forces during World War II. He had been shot down in Europe and captured by the Nazis, who kept him as a prisoner. Bill didn't know his father very well, but he was proud of him. If nothing else had come out of my time at Baker, my friendship with Bill Richardson would have been worth it. That's how much I valued him as a friend and still do to this day. Bill was a ray of hope and ultimately a lifeline during a pretty challenging time.

Nineteen seventy was a confusing and tumultuous year for me. On campus, if people were supporting the war, they'd want to hook up with me, and some of them vehemently thought I was going to be their champion. But I didn't much feel like spending time with them, let alone championing their cause. Baker was a church school in a pretty buttoned-up town, and there were laws saying you couldn't purchase or consume alcohol within a five-mile radius. If you wanted to go out drinking, you had to go out of town to do it, usually about eighteen miles north to Lawrence, home to the University of Kansas, a center of liberalism and antiwar activism.

So I'd drive up to Lawrence to see the real live hippies in their natural element. There was a lot going on at that time, not just on the University of Kansas campus, but on campuses across the country. Word was that with spring coming, there was going to be another national demonstration, like the October moratorium, and violence nationwide began to ratchet up. First came Kent State, when members of the Ohio National Guard fired on a group of student protesters, killing four and wounding nine others. At first I had heard there was a sniper, and the Guardsmen were returning fire, and my immediate thought was, *More power to them*. Then it became clear that there had not been a sniper, and from that point forward I only referred to what happened as the murders at Kent State. Eleven days later, in Jackson, Mississippi, city and state police opened fire on a group of black student protesters in a dormitory at Jackson State, killing two and wounding twelve. I saw photos of the dorm, and they had really shot the hell out of the place.

Following Kent State, the response on the Baker campus was very emotional, and the response on the University of Kansas campus was downright explosive. We heard that something was going to happen at Baker the next day, and I was in the student union when a group from KU came in, asking where they could find this Gunny Musgrave guy. Some people pointed them over to me, and a crowd of students followed them as they came my way. The students from KU said they were sent to tell me that elements from the Students for a Democratic Society, or SDS, a left-wing national student activist organization, were going to come to Baker, pull down the American flag, and burn it. And I thought, *How the fuck do these guys know who I am?* Also, there was no way I was going to permit that to happen, especially after they came to tell me about it in advance. But now I had all these Baker students circling round me going, "Ooooh. He's going to kill these guys." I looked intensely at the guy who had spoken to me and said, "Well, I appreciate the heads-up," and then asked him if he'd take a response back to the SDS. He said he would. "Tell them to come on down and I'll meet them at the flagpole and help them take the flag down," I said, "because they're going to have to stand on my body to get to it. They'd better come ready, because I'm ready to die for that flag." And they said, "Okay," and took off. I imagined this was going to provoke a response in the Baker students, who would rise to my defense, but no one said a fucking thing. Not a single person stepped up to help.

The next day, about an hour before the group from SDS was supposed to show up, I put on my jungle jacket and jungle boots and walked out to the flagpole at the administration building. (I left my Fuck-You Jacket at home, because I didn't want it to get torn up or stained with blood.) I wasn't feeling too good about what was about to go down, because it was pretty likely I'd get the shit kicked out of me, but it had to be done. I'd like to think that if I told someone else, he would have followed me out there and stood by my side, but I hadn't told anyone, and so I was standing out there all alone. Then out walked this stocky guy, Alan Miller. He had served as an infantry officer in Vietnam. Alan, Bill, and I buddied around and spent a lot of time together, so I should have known that he would be there that day. "Well, Gunny, are we going to get our asses kicked today?" he casually asked. "I think we probably are," I said. "Okay, let's do it," he said as he stepped up beside me and crossed his arms, to let the world know that he was there to stay.

About fifty yards away, a group of students had gathered to mourn the deaths of the kids who had been killed at Kent State. They were giving speeches and talking about the war and what their response should be as students. All of a sudden I looked up and saw a whole crowd of guys coming at us, and I thought, *Holy shit. There's a lot of them. This ain't going to take too long.* But it turned out they were from one of the fraternities, and when they got close enough, they told us they had our backs, which, of course, came as a great relief. Then the entire police department, which consisted of one officer named George Rebman, pulled up in his car and motioned me over. George was a really good man, a good small-town cop with the perfect small-town touch, but he wasn't to be underestimated. If you pissed him off, he'd end up in charge, one way or another. We'd had only a few brief, respectful interactions in the past, but I walked over to his vehicle and he said, "You doin' okay?" And I said, "Yeah." "Everybody there on your side?" he asked. "Yeah, thank God," I replied. "Well, listen," he said, "I heard about this shit, and I just want you to know that if anything goes down, as of right now I am deputizing you. You'll be the cop." I told him how much I appreciated the gesture but that I wasn't comfortable with the role. "Well, then don't worry about having any problems with the law if something takes place," he said. "I know why you're here, and I know you will avoid violence if possible." Then he said, "I'm going to be sitting right here, and I'll back you up." So, at this point, I was feeling pretty good, with George Rebman and the fraternity boys on my side. The SDS would have to send a whole hell of a bunch of their so-called revolutionaries down and they'd better bring a sack lunch, because it was going to take all day.

Of course, in the end, nobody showed up. It was all a bunch of hot air. But now that I had the support of the fraternity guys, I felt pretty secure, as if I weren't totally on my own. From that point forward, though, I tried my best to avoid any further conflict. I didn't join any organizations, and whenever someone approached me about joining something, I'd say, "Look, I've got my hands full here just trying to remember how to read and take notes." I did get approached that spring about a blood drive, called Blood for Peace, and I said, "Look, if you want to take blood and send it to the Vietcong or something, you're talking to the wrong guy." But when I was told the blood would be distributed to VA hospitals and low-income hospitals, I decided it was something I could support. I went out and spoke to many organizations and told them, "These students are really trying to do something good here, and I'd like to invite you to support us in any way that you can. Don't be thrown off by the title. The blood isn't going to the Vietcong." I threw myself into it and got lots of leaders and students to show up and donate their blood, and I got townspeople involved as well. I wasn't the only person out there pounding the pavement, but my involvement helped motivate other students to work the campus. I was doing it like a Marine NCO, making people look me in the eye if they were going to say no. This one student was walking by me, and I said, "Hey, come over here and sign up to donate blood." And the kid, who was being a smart-ass, said, "I can't do it. I got bad blood." "Bullshit," I said. "All you've got is a bad back." Somehow, what I said caught on and people around campus were saying, "If you don't give blood, you must have a bad back," and pretty soon we had filled the whole gymnasium with people who were giving blood. The blood drive was a huge success, largely because of how much I committed myself to it, but it was also the only cause I got involved with at the time.

During my first two years at Baker, I was struggling like hell, completely conflicted. Back at the dorm, while they held the draft lottery, I'd sit in the back of the room, while all of these guys sat on the edges of their seats worried they'd pull a bad number. And when one of them did, I'd start laughing at the top of my lungs. My heart was cold. I wasn't sympathetic at all. The whole thing was bullshit. *If the war ain't worth winning, then it ain't worth fighting.* I had come to hate that fucking war, because these kids were now being asked to die for a retreat. I had buddies in country, and I don't know how they did it. I don't understand how they could have endured the conditions over there, knowing that they were dying for nothing. The entire situation was disgraceful, and I could not figure out what to do or how to express my frustration without being co-opted by groups on the left or attacked by groups on the right. So I did my best to keep my mouth shut and kept drinking to numb the pain. People would ask me what I thought, and I'd give them the company line about being a Marine and supporting my buddies, but inside I was sick. I felt betrayed. The U.S. government had pissed on everything I thought I was fighting for. At least that's how I saw it at the time. Also, I was suffering from a horrible, unrelenting case of survivor's guilt, thinking that my good fortune and survival were burdens rather than gifts, because I didn't feel as if I deserved either. A mistake had been made. I should have died back in Con Thien, and I was being crushed under the weight of every death I had ever witnessed or that had ever touched me.

As time went by, and more kids and innocent civilians were killed, I slowly began turning against the war. I wasn't going to admit it to anyone. I just couldn't. I had become a hero to many of the people on campus who were for the war. So rather than deal with my inner conflict, I just drank more, and I stopped sleeping in the dorm at night. It was against the rules, but I couldn't sleep unless I had a weapon. I had to have it near me, because my sleep—what little I was able to get—was ravaged with nightmares, and I didn't feel safe without it. My first roommate ran out of our room in terror one night when he heard me screaming in my sleep. Another guy—named Don Brower, who became a trusted friend—offered to come live with me and switched rooms with my roommate. He didn't seem to care that I had a rifle with me, always by my side, as I slept. He always backed me up.

Eventually, I moved into a little trailer at the end of a dead-end street on the edge of a creek. I spent my nights alone, and I was dating my .45. Every night when I got home, stumbling drunk, I'd take out my .45 and embrace it. I'd press it up against my temple. I'd stick it under my chin and wonder, *Do I have the guts?* Unable to blow my brains out, I'd think even less of myself. In my eyes, I was a coward, and I was convinced I had nothing to live for. That's how much I was hurting. Thoughts of death and dying haunted me for all my waking hours and invaded my dreams, which were nearly all about the war. Fortunately,

Me with my dog Smack, who saved my life on many occasions.

I had dogs living with me in the trailer, named Smack and Montana, and they made me get up in the morning and stay sober long enough at night to feed them. The night that I finally decided it was time to end it, I had let the dogs out. They scratched and I lay the pistol down and went back to let them in. They were so glad to see me that it made me realize what I was about to do. I decided that if I really wanted to commit suicide, I could do it the next day. They gave me the companionship I so desperately needed, because, except for the buddies I trusted and went drinking with, I was pushing everyone else away, and I had never felt so alone.

I decided that maybe if I wrote my thoughts down, I might be able to unburden myself of them, and so I set out to write the great American war novel. But writing a book requires concentration, something I had very little of. I couldn't get my mind to settle for long enough to write a paragraph, let alone a chapter. Then I remembered some poems I had read in high school by the British World War I veterans Siegfried Sassoon and Wilfred Owen, which sent me to the college library in search of their work, along with the poetry of other veterans. I checked out a book of World War I poets, mostly British Soldiers, but also a Canadian named Robert Service. And then I remembered that nearly every Veterans Day as I was growing up, I would hear someone read a poem called "In Flanders Fields," by the Canadian physician and lieutenant colonel John McCrae, who fought in the Second Battle of Ypres in the Flanders region of Belgium during World War I. Returning to that poem and exploring the poetry of other combat veterans, I discovered writers who were dealing with the reality of combat with their words, and it inspired me to want to follow in their footsteps. So I started writing poems.

At first, I found it nearly impossible to finish anything I started. Writing poetry is really hard, but it's even harder when you're drinking all the time. Rather than writing whole poems, I tried just to put my thoughts on paper in a poetic form. To my surprise, this shit just started pouring out of me, and each time I did it, I felt a little bit better. These were thoughts I couldn't deal with. They were dealing with me, which was why I was playing with that pistol every fucking night. But instead of picking up my .45, I would pick up a pen and then hold the piece of paper out away from me, at arm's length, and it would feel as though I had put some distance between myself and these thoughts. It seemed kind of ridiculous and overly symbolic, but somehow it was enough for me to feel as if I had some control. Before I started writing poems, if you had told me that I might feel better if I tried to write everything down, I would have laughed in your face and said, "That's just bullshit." I had to discover it for myself. At first I fought it pretty hard, but what I discovered was that even if my poems weren't any good, they helped in ways that I didn't fully understand.

I first had the impulse to write poems soon after returning home, before any of this dawned on me. The first poem I tried to write was in 1968 at Quantico Naval Hospital. It was set to the tune of "When Johnny Comes Marching Home," a popular song from the Civil War. In the poem, I thought about all of the teenage girls whom those boys in Vietnam left behind when they died. We were seniors in high school when we went to the war, and our girlfriends were the same age or younger, and many of them were pregnant. So I wrote the poem from the perspective of a sixteen-year-old pregnant widow, burying the body of her eighteen-year-old Marine husband, and the chorus was "When Johnny was carried home." And one of the verses went,

> Over his corpse was laid the flag,
> a worthless red, white, and blue rag.

In writing the poem, I had surprised myself with what came up, as if from an undiscovered part of my own mind. I thought to myself, *You'd better be careful, or this could turn into a great anti-war anthem.* So I hid it away for years. The first time I ever participated in a poetry reading was decades later, during the Gulf War. One of my fellow Vietnam veterans, who knew I wrote poetry, pushed me to do it, and the first thing I read was my poem, "When Johnny was carried home." Fittingly, the first poem I ever wrote was the first poem I ever read in public, but it took more than twenty years for me to find the guts to do it. But when I was in college, living in that little trailer at the end of that dead-end street, I wrote those poems to survive, and they were for my eyes alone. I would come home, pick up my .45, set it on the table, and make myself write another poem. I couldn't think beyond the next day, so I would put one foot in front of the other and write a poem that would get me through the night.

CHAPTER 13

Joining the VVAW

Each January at Baker, we had a month when we didn't go to classes, but instead used the time to investigate a single subject that interested us. It was called interterm. Because of my black buddies in the Marine Corps, I decided that I should learn more about the civil rights movement. A black author named Claude Brown came to campus. He had written a best-selling autobiography about growing up in Harlem called *Manchild in the Promised Land,* which I had actually read, along with a collection of Dr. King's speeches, during my time on active duty in D.C. So when I met him on campus, we got to have lunch together, and I told him, "Hey, I read your book when I was in the Marine Corps," to which he said, "Wow, I've never heard that before from a white guy."

He was a great person, really open and funnier than hell, and so I told him, and any of the black students on campus who would listen, about my interest in learning more about the civil rights movement. This led me to sign up for a course with about ten other Baker students that took place for a couple of weeks in Kansas City. We visited churches in the inner city and met with ministers and social activists. Each of the groups would do a presentation on their work, at the end of which we'd be given an opportunity to ask if we could come work with them. The only group that appealed to me, of all of the groups we met, was the Black Panthers, because they had a clear mission and weren't afraid to arm and defend themselves. In many ways, they reminded me of the Marine Corps. The founder of the Kansas City chapter was a guy named Pete O'Neal, and I asked to speak with him. I was wearing a field jacket and still had short hair and knew how strange it looked, but I went right over to him, looked him in the eye, and in my southern accent said, "Can I work with you? You're the only one here that I know for sure is helping kids." I had been impressed to learn that the Black Panthers had developed a number of social programs, including one offering free breakfast for underserved children. "Hell yeah," he said. "You think you got what it takes?" And I said, "Well, as a matter of fact, I think I do." So he told me to come with him, and we got into a beat-up old Volkswagen and drove into a rough section of Kansas City. Normally, it would have been dangerous for me to be in this part of town, but I was with him, so it was cool.

As we approached the building where the Black Panthers were holding their meeting, he pointed up in the sky and said, "Do you see that helicopter?" and sure enough there was a helicopter hovering overhead. "Keep an eye on him. They painted something on the roof of my car. It's invisible. I can't see it, but they can, through a special lens." Then he proceeded to zigzag all over the inner city, driving down alleys, weaving in and out of traffic, and sure enough the helicopter stayed on us. "Well,

I'll be damned," I said, "you're right," and we both had a good laugh.

When we walked into the Black Panthers headquarters, everyone stood up and went, "Who the fuck are you?" Obviously, I was a cop, with my short hair and military look. O'Neal spoke up for me, telling everyone I was good and to calm down. His little brother was one of the organizers, and if he said someone was okay, then everyone else fell in line. He walked right up to me and shook my hand, and that was it. A couple of the other guys were retired Marines and Vietnam vets, and they came over and we did the whole vet thing—who you were with and when you were there—so they made sure we weren't bullshitting each other. And from then on, I had allies, and I spent the rest of my time there working with the Panthers, and it was a great experience.

I made sure they knew that I understood they were taking a big chance on me, and I also caught on pretty quickly. The organization was set up with a military-type hierarchy, a chain of command, and they conducted themselves like troops. When you joined, you were a turd, just like in the Corps, and you had to prove yourself. Of course, they weren't going to show me anything they didn't want me to see, but everything I saw those guys doing was impressive. They had writing programs for kids, nursery programs, and adult learning programs. My entire time there was super positive, and I developed a real sense of admiration for the organization, which never felt preachy or caught up in the religious rhetoric of much of the civil rights movement. People in Kansas City were amazed when they saw me walking around with the Panthers, and it cemented my reputation forever when I got back to Baker and told people about it. My classmates couldn't believe it. I had been used to dealing

*Photos showing my short hair taken in Kansas City when I volunteered
to assist the Black Panther school breakfast program.*

with ultimate realities, so when the opportunity to work with
the Black Panthers arose, it felt as if anything else would have
been a waste of time. Those guys had guts, and they were doing
something that felt as though it cut right to the heart of the
civil rights issue. And they were getting attacked all over the
country. There were assassinations set up on the leadership of
the Black Panther Party all the time. While I was working at
their headquarters in Kansas City, there was a hit on a leader in
Chicago, Fred Hampton. Even Pete O'Neal, the chairman of
the Kansas City chapter, had to flee the country, to Algeria and
then Tanzania, not long after I met him, in order to avoid being
locked up. If you want to neuter an organization, take out the
leadership; that was the strategy toward activists and organizations the government wanted to dismantle. Needless to say, I
learned a great deal during my short time working with them

that January. I came to the conclusion that it was going to take a lot more than singing "We Shall Overcome" to turn the tide. Spending time with the Black Panthers showed me that racist policies were so entrenched in American life that they weren't going to be overcome without struggle. These men and women were not anything like how they were being portrayed in the press, and—as a Marine Vietnam veteran—I understood their anger, and I admired their discipline and their willingness to sacrifice. They knew the government was at war with them.

By the time I returned to Baker, I had decided that the war was ridiculous, and I had become very critical of it. I had begun to see that it was an unjust war, in which millions of innocent people had died, and that the government had been wrong from the very beginning. But I still harbored the fear that I was going to betray my buddies. A lot of Vietnam veterans I knew would say, "I think the war sucks, but I'm not going to stab my friends in the back," and I could relate to them.

Later that year—it was December 1970—while reading *Playboy* magazine, I turned to a page on which there was a photograph of a flag-covered casket. It was an advertisement by an organization that I'd never heard of called Vietnam Veterans Against the War, and it was addressed to veterans like me. It said something like "If you want to stop the war you fought in, then send in this card." None of the appeals by people in the so-called peace movement had ever reached me. I wasn't about to associate myself with the people who had treated me like trash when I came home. They wanted me to speak out at their rallies. They told me my voice was important. Well, I hadn't been good enough for them when I came home, so I sure as hell wasn't good enough for them now. But the VVAW was different. The appeal was coming from a group of veterans, and it caught me off guard. I sent in the little card, and the VVAW mailed me back a whole bunch of information about how the government was denying that we had invaded Laos and were waging a secret war there, in spite of overwhelming evidence to the contrary. They were announcing their first national demonstration in D.C., to call out the government for lying to the American people about Laos, and I thought, *It's time to get up off my ass and start doing something. I know the war is wrong, and dying for a retreat is horseshit. I'm a fucking coward and unworthy of the title of "Marine," which I value so much, if I'm not willing to take some kind of a risk and make a statement to the American people about this war and our conduct in it now.* So I decided to go to D.C.

Before making the trip, though, I felt that I had to call my buddies that I was still in touch with and tell them what I was doing, because they were my brothers and I needed them to know what I was planning. So I called each of them and said, "I just want you to know what I'm doing and why I'm doing it." A couple of them thought I was wrong and were angry with me. They warned me I would be making a big mistake and told me not to do it. "I don't have a choice," I told them. "I've got to do it. This war is ridiculous now, and I cannot stand on the sidelines and feel like I'm still worthy of respect. I'm a citizen, and citizens have to choose sides. If I don't, I'm nothing." I also told them, "I didn't call to ask your permission. I called to tell you why I'm doing it." A few were supportive and said things like "Good for you, but I'm scared for you." One of the guys to whom I owe my life, Dan Cooney, just sighed and said, "Goddamn it. When are you going to be there?" "I plan on arriving the day before the thing kicks off," I told him. "Okay," he said. "Let's meet at the Marine Memorial in Arlington." And I said, "Well, wait a minute, Dan, I'm just calling to let you know

Me and Dan Cooney, both on crutches, at Dan's farm in Maryland. Dan was with me in 1-9 at Con Thien. He saved my life and always took good care of me. At Khe Sanh, he stepped on a mine. It screwed up his right foot pretty bad.

that I'm doing it." "Last time I let you out of my sight for five minutes, you got your ass shot off," he said. "If you're going to march in Washington, D.C., I'm going to be beside you," and he walked off his job and alienated his entire family by going to meet me in Washington, D.C.

The night before the demonstration, I waited for Dan at the Marine Memorial in Arlington Cemetery, and when he arrived, I knew everything was going to be okay, because he was there with me. When he found me, Dan said, "Hey, we were together in the war, and we'll be together in the antiwar." He showed up, risking everything that was stable in his life, just to back me up. That is a FRIEND in capital letters. That is a singular kind of love. So we marched together for the first time against the war, and it meant a lot to me. Though I met guys that week who would end up being friends for the rest of my life, Dan was the only person I knew at the demonstration. When we showed up the next morning, we were told to look for people who put up signs for their organizations or the units they were in. I found the Kansas City Vietnam Veterans Against the War group, and the guy in charge, Johnie Upton, was this little tiny squid who had been a Navy corpsman, or enlisted medical specialist, with the Recon Marines. This guy was hard-core. He was disabled, but clearly nothing was going to stop him. I hung close with him throughout the week, and it changed my life. I became a wholehearted supporter of the VVAW, which was composed mostly of combat veterans at the time I joined. To my surprise, there were also a lot of cops in the movement. In those days, they would give guys a six-month "early out" of the military if they signed up to be police officers in major cities. So we were running into all of these cops in D.C. who were lifting up their ties and on the bottom on the backside were pins that said, "I support Vietnam Veterans Against the War." They would bring us coffee and donuts in the morning and tell us, "Don't worry, we've got your back, brother."

We took over the area of the National Mall that's closest to the Capitol, and Nixon said he wanted us gone and ordered us to disperse. I met a lot of congressmen who came down to hang out with us, and some of them were combat vets from World War II and the Korean War. The VVAW got a bunch of high-powered lawyers to file a lawsuit about our constitutional right to gather on the mall, and it was fast-tracked right to the Supreme Court. All the while, we stayed out there, shouting, "Hell no, we won't go!" It was the first time Vietnam vets were saying this. Ramsey Clark, who had been the attorney general while I was in the Marine Corps and was now our lawyer, came out to see us on the day the case was to be heard by the Supreme Court and said, "They'll rule against us, and then you guys will have to decide what you are going to do. Because by five o'clock they're going to come down here and arrest you if you do not vacate the mall." So the leadership got together, guys like John Kerry, Al Hubbard, and Skip Roberts, who later became friends of mine. They were all on the national steering committee at the time, and they said to us that we had to meet with our groups and decide what we were going to do. When the time came, were we going to surrender and walk off the mall? Or were we going to make them arrest us?

All of the groups met and debated what to do. This was a democratic movement, and some of the guys in my group said, "We've got to fight these motherfuckers." And I said, "But what if these cops out here support us? Most of them are Vietnam vets. I'm not going to fight a fellow veteran, but I ain't going to leave either." The consensus among the groups was to stay and resist nonviolently. This was a strategic position. We were warriors who were not afraid to defend ourselves, if necessary, but as representatives of a national organization it made more sense for us to practice nonviolence. No matter what happened, we would not raise a hand against a police officer or a National Guardsman. And when the court decision came down, the order said that if we slept or made preparations to sleep on the mall, then we could be arrested. So we set our alarms for the appointed hour, resumed chanting, "Hell no, we won't go!," and braced ourselves for the impending conflict. We waited for the cops, but they didn't show up. We waited for the National Guard, and they didn't show up, either. By then it was getting dark, and people started walking up onstage, asking if they could speak to us. The chief of police was told by one of his cops in the D.C. Metropolitan Police Department, "If you're telling me to go in there and start gassing and clubbing disabled veterans and throwing them in the back of our paddy wagons, I don't think most of my officers are going to follow my order." A group of the National Guardsmen who were called up for riot duty that night appeared on the mall. One of them came over to us and said, "I just want you to know that when we were called up tonight, we told our commanding officers, 'If you order us to fix our bayonets against our brothers on the mall, we will throw down our rifles and join them.'" He said they were immediately disbanded and were now there on the mall to be arrested with us.

It was fucking beautiful. We had been treated like shit ever since we came home, and now we had the police department on our side, and these incredible active-duty Soldiers who had our backs. We were all giddy with excitement, and as we unrolled our sleeping bags on the lawn, we made a big show of it, yawning and snoring as loudly as we could, just daring them to come get us. But nobody made a move, and the cops told us not to worry. They weren't going to bother us. The chief of police finally told his men they weren't going to do a fucking thing. If Nixon wants to get those guys out of there, he told his men, then he's going to have to do it himself. We spent the rest of the week out there, and no one lifted a finger to stop us. It was exhilarating.

The first day of the demonstration, we had marched from our station areas, across the Potomac River, over the bridge that goes by the Lincoln Memorial, where the Vietnam Veterans Memorial now sits. We marched past the mall, past the Washington Monument, all the way to the Capitol, where we camped. On our way there, we marched by Arlington National Cemetery, and when we tried to enter so we could be with our fallen brothers, we were met by armed guards who blocked us at the main gates. There was nearly a riot, and the VVAW leadership had to work like maniacs to keep us all from going nuts. They told us that if we tried to break in, there would be violence, and we would not be honoring our brothers that way. They said our dead brothers would be ashamed of us, and that's how they got us to leave. We didn't turn away from those gates because our government was telling us to go. Every single one of us was willing to die to get through that goddamn gate, but the Arlington staff reasoned with us and so did the VVAW leadership, and we moved on and marched onto the mall and set up our camp.

But the next day, we decided, we would march back to Arlington National Cemetery and we would climb over the fence, if we had to, to be with our dead brothers. So, the next day, we marched to Arlington, and when we got there, knowing we were serious and not wanting any trouble, they opened the gates for us, and when we marched in, there was a funeral going on, down in the valley. We were absolutely quiet and respectful as we marched down past it and then up a road, which curved up a hill, where we planned to go to soothe our grief. As we walked through those gates, a bugler started to play taps, and when the sound hit my ears, I just started crying. And when I started, I couldn't stop. It was horrible. Everything I had been holding back rose up and hit me right there, and I fell to the ground sobbing and I couldn't lift myself. I just knelt there on the soil of Arlington uncontrollably weeping. A group of Vietnam veterans, guys I didn't know, came over, picked me up, carried me to a Jeep, and drove me back to the mall. They weren't going to leave their wounded. That was the day that I found my new unit. I was wounded, and they came back and got me out. From that point forward, I committed everything to the VVAW. I resolved to see this through to the end. They could put me in prison for it. They could kill me. But they couldn't stop me. That day in Arlington National Cemetery, I took my oath of enlistment.

When I left for D.C., I hadn't told my folks about what I was doing, because I still wasn't sure how I felt about it. I didn't know if I was going to stay the whole week or if I would, upon seeing how things were on the ground, turn right around and come home. Several days into the demonstration, word began to spread around D.C. that we planned to deliver our war medals to Congress in a body bag. So they put up a fence to block us from the Capitol steps, which pissed off the VVAW organizers, who then set up our microphones at the base of the fence, where dozens of reporters from all over the world had gathered to hear what we were going to say. Then every veteran who wanted to speak was invited to come up to the microphones, make a statement, and throw his shit over the fence. This was to be the grand finale of our demonstration, and it turned out to be a lot more impressive than anyone expected. The line of veterans waiting to speak snaked back hundreds of yards. I found my place toward the back and waited my turn, wearing my green dress jacket with all of my ribbons on it; most of us were wearing parts of our uniforms. I had started letting my hair grow in the fall of 1970. There was no real plan. It just happened. I wasn't making a statement, at first. But I did purposely grow my beard, and eventually I let both grow so long that it became part of my in-your-face attitude. With my appearance, I was saying to the world, "Just because my hair is long and I have a beard, doesn't change who I am or where I've been or what I've been through. It's just how I choose to look now."

One reporter, who happened to be a Marine, sought me out in the line and asked me a bunch of questions. I didn't think anything of it at the time. We were just talking and shooting the shit, and then I went up and made my statement: "The main thing that I wish I could return," I said, holding up my medals and pointing at the Capitol, "are the lives I took in their name," and then threw my medals over the fence. By discarding our medals, we wanted America to realize just how serious we were. The reporter wrote an article about me that went out via United Press International, and it ended up being published in the local newspaper back home.

My parents, who had no idea I was in D.C., heard me make my statement over the radio while on a trip to Colorado Springs. They were shocked, to say the least. My dad was not particularly understanding about the whole thing, until he got home and found out that there had been some threats made against me in the community. I was told that people felt that

I had "thrown away their medals" and said they were going to come over to get me. My decorations had been a front-page story when I came home, because I was one of the first guys in the neighborhood to receive military awards and still be alive. So I guess some members in the community felt they had some ownership over those awards. When the article came out with my statement and listed the awards I had chucked over the Capitol fence, it pissed a lot of people off. The article was called "Local Vet a Protestor." When I came home to talk with my parents about it, I thought I was going to be in for some real arm wrestling about what I had done. Dad said, "Look, I don't understand this. And I don't like it. But you know what you're doing. I just wish you'd found a different way to make your point. But it's your point and you make it the way you want to make it. And anybody who thinks they're going to give you shit about this, we'll go to bat with them out in the driveway."

My father never did become comfortable with my being in the VVAW or the peace movement, so we just didn't talk about it. To the outside world, the Musgraves had closed ranks. It was "us against them," as far as we were concerned, and I remember my father on a number of occasions coming to my defense and saying to people, "You don't have shit to say about this. Those weren't your medals."

Even people back home who knew me well were shocked by what I did. Many of my old friends had admired me for going into the Corps right out of high school, and they had been hesitant to say anything against the war out of loyalty to me, especially after I got wounded. These same friends were confused when they learned I had joined the VVAW. They didn't know how to react. I was accused by some of being a traitor, a communist, and a "chickenshit," but other people asked, "What took you so long?" One World War II couple that we knew very well had a really hard time with my joining the VVAW. Whenever I saw them, they would say, "What are we supposed to think? What are we supposed to feel, when you do this?" And I'd say, "Well, how do you think I feel? I didn't want to do this, but I don't have a choice. This is my war and I have to make a stand." When people asked me how I could join the antiwar movement, I'd tell them, "It was the hardest decision of my life." Inside, I was still struggling. By joining the antiwar movement, I had hurt my folks and other family members. I hurt people I loved. And I lost some of the hard-won respect I had earned from the World War II vets who were my heroes. It would have been a lot easier to have just kept my mouth shut, but this was bigger than me.

CHAPTER 14

Public Speaking

RIGHT AFTER RETURNING FROM D.C., I started gaining more responsibility and quickly rose through the ranks. I also got a lot of speaking requests. I had just gone public, but soon found myself in the role of state coordinator and then regional coordinator, and soon thereafter spokesman. All of a sudden people wanted to hear what I had to say, because they knew who I was. Schools invited me regularly to come speak with their students, and I said yes to every invitation. I didn't feel I had the right to say no. I was asked to do more and more press, and once I'd been interviewed in newspapers, and the Associated Press and United Press International wires had picked up the stories, my name was added to a series of reference lists kept by newspapers on subjects related to the war. In the beginning, the primary question was, "Is the war right or wrong?" but eventually I started getting asked to talk about Agent Orange or the psychological wounds of the war. If the VVAW headquarters got an interview request for anything based in the Midwest, they'd immediately bounce it down to me.

I found I was good at giving interviews, but I felt pretty exposed opening myself up to the American people. I committed myself 100 percent to the cause, but wasn't fully prepared for the consequences. Because the best defense is a very aggressive offense, adversarial groups started to invite me to speak in order to attack me. I showed up to one small town in Kansas, where I was told I had been invited to speak by a Methodist youth group. When I got to this church, out in the middle of nowhere, before I stepped out of the car, I saw that the church was packed and the parking lot filled with pickup trucks, and I realized I wasn't going to be talking to kids. The entire town was waiting for my ass. I had just met this girl, whom I had brought along for the gig. She was sitting in the passenger seat, and I handed her the keys and said, "Look, if this goes bad, you get to the car and get out of here. Don't worry about me. I don't even want you to look backward. Just get out of here, and then go call for help."

This time, I was pretty sure they were going to beat the shit out of me right there in the parking lot, as soon as they saw me step out in my jungle jacket with my long hair and beard. But I got out of the car all the same, and I walked up to the church as if I were in command. When I entered, I saw that I had a choice of where to sit, so I crossed over and sat right under a giant picture of Jesus, because one of the first questions I always got hit with was, "Why do you have long hair?" Pointing up at the picture of Jesus, I'd say, "What would you do if he walked in here wearing a jungle jacket and started talking to you about peace? Would you ask him why his hair was long? Would you accuse him of being un-American? Or would you take the time to give him the benefit of the doubt and listen to what he had to say?" Speaking as someone who was raised in the church and appealing to congregations as a Christian often defused tough situations. I'd try to address the tension in the room up front and would kick things off by saying, "I've got a feeling you've got a lot of questions for me. Who wants to start?" A lot of times, rather than speaking at audiences, I'd simply let them ask me questions. It never seemed right to simply make my statement and then head for the door. All of those people were crammed into that damn church because they had something on their minds and they needed to talk to somebody about it, and by the end of the evening, if I had done my job well, they were talking with me. I'm not saying they all agreed with me. I'm not sure if I changed anyone's mind, but I did convince them I deserved respect, on a personal level, and that I wasn't a radical. I might have had long hair and a beard, but I was still the same kid who had carried the rifle in the jungle. These were working-class families I was talking to, and when I spoke with them about the injustice of the war and the way the government was waging it with a poor man's body count, it gave them something to think about that many of them had not contemplated before. I also spoke about the staggering numbers of innocent civilians who had died in North and South Vietnam, now known to total more than two million. *Were these the values of the Christian church?* I tried to bring them inside my thought process as I slowly began to question the war, looking for justifications of our presence in Vietnam and finding none that seemed to stand up to scrutiny.

One of the things that always happened, and I still thank God for it, is that there would often be Vietnam veterans in the audience; they were always the first ones to come up and shake my hand. I think they knew what they were doing, showing all their neighbors that they considered me a brother and that no one had to defend them from me, because I had their respect, and the respect was mutual. One of the most basic responsibilities of a citizen in a democracy is to question our government and hold it accountable, rather than kissing its ass and saying, "My country right or wrong." The most patriotic thing we can do as citizens is to say no to our government when we think it isn't representing the people in the best possible way. Once audiences got past my appearance and heard what I was saying, spoken to them in their own language, they opened up a bit and gave me a fair shake. "Silence is consent," I'd tell them. And I'd also say, "I want to be wrong. I want one of you in this audience to change my mind, convince me that everything I went through really meant something, convince me that we need to be there, that we need to have young American poor and working-class kids dying in a jungle eight thousand miles from here for a retreat. Please convince me, because I don't like doing this, and, unfortunately, I am certain you are not going to be able to do it, because I didn't just wake up this morning and decide, *Oh, I think I'm going to be against the war today.* It was a long, slow, horribly painful process that had me studying my ass off trying to find the justification that I needed that would support my soul and allow me not to have to be involved. But I couldn't find it, because it wasn't there. It was all bullshit."

So on that night at the church in the small Kansas town, like many others, people showed up hostile and defensive but went away inviting me to come back and talk with their young people again. This was always a tremendous personal victory for me, because rather than peeling out of the parking lot in reverse or running for my life, I faced my fears. It was a different kind of combat, and the stakes seemed just as high. I knew I could get hurt, maybe even killed, doing it, because when you talk about war, you are always going to elicit heightened emotions from people, and it's going to get heated. Lives were at stake. The future of our country and democracy hung in the balance.

My greatest fear, far greater than being kicked to shit by an angry mob who saw me as a symbol of everything they hated—rebels, traitors, hippies—was to be met with scorn by other Vietnam veterans who would call me a communist or a buddy fucker. That was the absolute worst, being called a buddy fucker—as in someone who fucked over his buddies—but eventually I realized that I had to accept that some veterans would view me that way. Ninety percent of my interactions with fellow Vietnam veterans ended well, and that was primarily because I was a grunt. If I had been a clerk typist, I don't think it would have gone as well, but being a disabled grunt commanded a certain respect that most people have for warriors who have been wounded doing their job. Because of this, people gave me just enough slack that I was able to speak my mind. There were so many activists out there spewing philosophical, political bullshit that most midwesterners tuned out the antiwar movement, but when they saw a wounded veteran trying to speak his truth, people would sometimes open themselves to the possibility of what he was saying. I tried to tell people that being patriotic didn't always mean blind allegiance to a set of rules established by politicians in Washington. I did my best to show people that there was more than one definition of the word and that it was bigger than just saying yes to the president.

With increasingly frequent speaking engagements and greater leadership roles came more responsibility. When I wore the Marine Corps uniform, I knew that when people looked at me, they didn't see John D. Musgrave, they saw a U.S. Marine, and they weren't going to judge my actions in a vacuum. They were going to judge every Marine by what I did and said. When

I wore the uniform, I represented the entire Corps, and when I wore the VVAW badge on my jacket, I was representing thousands of other Vietnam veterans, and I had to conduct myself in a way that honored them all. So that was a heavy mantle to wear, and I met a lot of guys in the VVAW who were serving themselves—raising their own profiles in the media and public eye—rather than serving their country and their fellow veterans. They were feathering their nests, as we said, by wearing the badge. When the government increased the pressure on us, compelling us to take greater risks in order to remain in the organization, these were the guys who renounced the VVAW as quickly as they could. In particular, threat of grand jury indictments intimidated those who were in it for themselves. It was similar to what we saw in the peace movement after the draft lottery came out. If guys had high numbers, they dropped out of the movement, which spoke volumes about why they were involved. When the indictments started coming down on the VVAW, the weaker members quit in droves, and the government counted on it.

The government was afraid of the VVAW and considered us a serious threat, because we were the only people speaking out against the war that most people in Nixon's "silent majority" would take seriously. I once read that we were the most infiltrated organization in the peace movement. We had undercover government agents among our ranks and also people we called Trots (communists who believed in the teachings of the Soviet revolutionary Leon Trotsky) sowing seeds of discord within the VVAW and the peace movement. The Trots' primary strategy was to co-opt demonstrations and make them appear as if they were their own. The Trots would throw their support behind student rallies, whipping up the students' excitement, and then, when the students were met with force by the police, they'd throw bricks at the cops, provoking them to sweep in and beat the shit out of all the students. Then they'd tell the students they were helping them "become revolutionaries." These were some of their tactics, which were aimed at fueling internal division and destabilizing the movement.

We were also very heavily bugged, so the feds could listen to our meetings with the hope of hearing someone say, "I think we ought to attack and kill these people," or "We should start guerrilla warfare," or "Let's start our own covert Phoenix program here in the States." Most of the time, though, it was just the guys on the government's payroll who said those kinds of things at meetings. The goal of the Department of Justice in the late 1960s and early 1970s was to emasculate the movement, by any means necessary. One of the most effective ways they accomplished this was through grand juries. They would haul you before one to answer the government's questions. Your lawyer would not be allowed in the room, but the government could have a whole battery of lawyers there, who would be firing questions at you that could not be asked in an open courtroom, such as "Can you tell us about every meeting you've been to in the past twelve months where antiwar activities were planned? What are the names of everyone who was there, and what did they say?" Questions like that are called "grand fishing expeditions," and they are not admissible in an actual court of law. But in a grand jury, they can ask questions like that. Of course, you can refuse to answer them, and the government will then threaten you with criminal contempt, which is a federal violation and can get you jailed for the life of the grand jury, which could be up to eighteen months. So they used that threat to compel you to answer their questions, and you could rack up quite a bit of time in prison for just sitting there and refusing to answer. Sometimes, you might immediately be jailed, right there, on the spot. Marshals would take you off the witness stand and lock you in a cell.

The other big strategy the government used to undermine the movement was the charge of conspiracy. For example, if I decided that I was going to get in an airplane and fly low over a town and throw out antiwar literature, I could be arrested for littering, but if I talked to the pilot about it, or if I had friends helping me load the plane, then I've created a conspiracy to litter. Littering itself is a misdemeanor, but conspiracy is a felony. So they didn't really give a shit if we'd done anything wrong, because with a conspiracy charge they could bring us in front of a grand jury and usually get an indictment. That's what they did to us in early 1972 down in Gainesville, Florida, when they brought seven members of the VVAW and a civilian who worked in a hardware store before a grand jury and charged them with conspiracy to overthrow the Republican National Convention in Miami Beach that summer.

First they said we planned to use wrist rocket slingshots to fire fried marbles at the police. I didn't even know you could fry a marble, but evidently you can, and then it shatters on impact. Later they charged us with planning to hide car bombs under our bell-bottom pants and also to place these bombs in the gas tanks of Miami Beach police cars and blow them up. I remember one of our defense lawyers countering these charges by saying, "It looks like the only thing they are not going to be doing at this convention is using nuclear weapons." As the convention approached and we got closer to our trial date, the government kept concocting more of these preposterous charges. They ended up putting a handful of our members in jail for contempt

I'm protesting at the 1972 Republican National Convention in Miami Beach.
Photo credit: Jean-Pierre Laffont.

when they refused to answer questions, and that's when they emasculated us and we stopped being an effective antiwar organization. Instead of focusing on demonstrating against the war, we had to direct the majority of our energies toward keeping our members out of prison, which meant that instead of asking people to donate to marches in Washington, we were asking them to donate to our defense fund.

Right before the trial, the Republican National Convention took place. I was appointed director of security on the VVAW campsite in Miami Beach. One of the biggest and most vocal groups demonstrating at the convention was the Youth International Party, called Yippies, whose political platform was "Free Drugs for Everybody." Also, there was breakaway faction of the Yippies called Zippies, which stood for the "Zeitgeist International Party" run by a guy named Tom Forcade, the founder of

High Times magazine. We didn't know exactly what they were up to at the time, but we knew enough to protect ourselves, individually and as an organization, because anything we did or were associated with doing could be used to put our buddies in prison for a long time. So my job was to help shield us from all of the other organizations in the peace movement that had come down to protest in Miami. I was sent down there early for us to stake out an area in Flamingo Park for just the VVAW. We had our own security, and we wouldn't let anyone into our campsite who wasn't a member of the VVAW or vouched for by a member. There were thousands of people down there, and we spent most of our time and energy working to ensure that we wouldn't be brought down by someone else doing something stupid, for which we would be blamed.

Then the National Socialist White People's Party, formerly known as the American Nazi Party, showed up on the scene, and things took a turn for the worse. There was a communal area called Expo '72, where an open truck trailer had been turned into a stage. We were not allowed to restrict access to the park, and so anyone who had something to say could climb up on that stage with a megaphone and say whatever the hell he wanted to say. When the Nazis showed up, there was a small woman onstage talking about women's rights. The Nazis split up and entered from multiple points, all at once, without their armbands on, and converged on the stage, where they attempted to take the megaphone away from the woman, but she fought them and wouldn't let go of it. They ended up throwing her off the trailer, but she took the megaphone with her, and all of a sudden a flood of people came running into the VVAW camp. All of these activists, who had spent plenty of time criticizing us, were begging us to get rid of the Nazis. So a bunch of us got up and rushed over to the Expo '72 area and, sure enough, the Nazis were there, marching around with their swastika armbands, yelling, "Sieg Heil" and "Death to the Jews."

We put up a cordon on the stage, separating the Nazis from the nonviolent peaceniks, who now began talking enormous amounts of trash in the direction of the Nazis. Then people in the crowd started throwing big tall cans of beer, and some of the Nazis started battering up against my vets. I was down front trying to negotiate with these guys and to get them out but wasn't making much progress, so a few of us went over to the police and asked them to come in and help us. But the police said that they had worked out an agreement with us that we were going to govern what took place in Flamingo Park, where we had set up a camp. "If we go in there now to take the Nazis out," one of them said, "we're also going to arrest everybody we see smoking dope." *Well, shit,* we thought, *we can't have that.* That was 80 percent of the people in the movement. So we went back in with the knowledge that we were going to have to take care of the situation ourselves. The peace movement was telling us to get them out, and the cops told us, "We'll be out here waiting for you. Bring them to us and we'll handle it, but you've got to take care of it in there."

One Nazi approached me and said, "Look, brother, I'm a Vietnam vet. I'm pretty sure you can get us out of here, because the crowd is starting to get ugly." And I said, "First of all, what the hell are you doing up there? You ought to be down here with us. That's number one. And number two, yeah, we'll get you out of here, but you've got to do as we say." He told me they would leave only if we agreed to their demands, which were simple. Only national socialist songs could be sung, and only national socialist flags could be flown, and only national socialist slogans could be spoken from the stage. If we committed to that, he told me, they'd leave. To which I replied, "Yeah. You're out of your fucking mind. Do you want to live, or do you want to die? Because we're going to let these people have you if you don't step off this stage." We gave them a few minutes, by the end of which we told them, "You are either going to walk out of here protected by us, or we're going to drag you out, because we can't hold this crowd back much longer." When the allotted time ran out, one of our young combat vets, a kid from Miami, stepped up onto the truck stage, took one of the Nazis by the arm, and said, "Come on, buddy, let's go." The Nazi reached down, grabbed a metal chair, and swung it around, hitting him square in the face, breaking his nose and shattering his glasses, and for the rest of the fight, which then erupted, the veteran was on the ground but hanging on to the Nazi with both of his arms and not letting go. Upon seeing this, the crowd transformed into an angry, murderous mob, and the whole thing descended into an all-out brawl. We had to beat the Nazis into submission and then fight our way through the mob to get them out of there alive, because the mob wanted to kill them. Those little Mahatma Gandhis were out for blood. So we had to push through the sea of people. Once we made it through, the crowd would part, and we'd toss each of these guys individually out onto the street, where the cops would be all over them. They arrested all of those Nazis and hauled them off to jail, and Clarence Kelley, who was chief of the Kansas City Police Department and later the FBI and was in charge of security down at the convention, issued the VVAW a letter of thanks, along with the mayor, for taking care of the Nazis. At the same time we were being indicted for conspiracy to disrupt the convention with violence, we were being commended by convention security for averting mob action through our direct intervention.

On the last day of the demonstrations, they flew Huey gunships over the park, surveying us closely—you can tell a gun-ship by the rocket pods on each side and the chin guns on the front—hoping to catch us doing something that could bolster their charges against us before we dispersed. At this point, they were trying everything they could to undermine and disman-tle the VVAW. Those of us in leadership decided it would be best if we left before the last night, to avoid any possibility of trouble, but some of my members said, "We want to stay," and I told them, "Feel free to stay, but understand you'll be staying as individuals and not as part of this organization." And they said, "Fine, we understand," which meant that I couldn't go, because I wasn't going to leave them behind. So I ended up staying with them, and it got pretty hairy on that last night, when the helicopters swooped in and sprayed tear gas all over the park, which was surrounded by elderly people holed up in apartments with air conditioners that sucked in the air from the outside. They were gassing Holocaust survivors, which became appar-ent when many of the residents came to the park to ask for our assistance with the tear gas. All I wanted to do was get my people out of there and for us not to get arrested. Miraculously, we made it out unscathed, but it was a difficult night for me, because I didn't have the organization to back me up. I was on my own in a country that was at war with us and that would send us to prison for being citizens exercising our First Amend-ment rights.

Right after the Republican convention came the VVAW trial, and we mobilized as many people as we could to come to Gainesville to be present for it and to make our voices heard. Lots of big names in the antiwar movement came down to lock arms with us and demonstrate as the trial was taking place. Anthony Russo, one of the leakers of the Pentagon Papers, was there, and Pete Seeger gave a wonderful concert on the University of Florida campus. His health wasn't so good at the time, but he delivered an amazing performance, which brought everyone together.

The judge of the trial issued a gag ruling, which meant that if we said anything about the trial, we could be arrested and put in jail. To minimize our exposure during the trial, the organization chose two spokesmen so we could control what was said to the press. I was number one, and Bart Savage from Chicago was my backup. That way, we wouldn't say anything that could get our members arrested, unless we had to. At the first press conference we held, I talked only about logistics: "On Monday, we're going to do this, and on Tuesday we'll try this." That was all I said to the reporters. "If you want to get stories," I told them, "this is where we'll be." Well, this is when I discovered that the guy who writes headlines at a newspaper is different from the guy who writes stories. The next day, a national story ran about what I had said. The story itself was completely accurate, but the headline read, "Vietnam Veterans Defy Judge's Gag Rule." And so I got grabbed by the police and brought before the court. The judge asked me, "Are you out there violating my gag rule?" And I said, "No, sir. I am not. If you read the article, you will see that I didn't say anything that was in violation of your gag rule." The judge was a good old boy, a southern gentleman named Winston Arnow, and he was simply a puppet for the Justice Department. "Your Honor," I said, "please read the article. It's not that long. I didn't say anything out of line." But he refused to read the article and said, "I know what you've done, and you're not going to change my mind." I couldn't believe this was actually happening and said, "Your Honor, I'd like to say one thing." And he said, "Be careful about it." "I just want you to understand that this issue is bigger than you and bigger than this courtroom. This is about freedom of speech, and we fought for it and take it really seriously." Judge Arnow looked down at me from his bench and said, "If you violate my gag rule one more time—" "I haven't violated it yet," I interjected. "If you violate it one more time, I am going to issue a warrant for your arrest."

A few days later, we physically caught the FBI in a broom closet of the federal courthouse, putting wiretaps on the phone terminals, which was totally illegal. They were not allowed to tap phones in the defense room of a court that promises to protect confidential conversations. There was a whole crowd of us in the defense room, attorneys and defendants, having a strategy conversation, when one of my fellow VVAW members pointed at an air vent and said, with total disbelief, "Look at that." All of a sudden we saw these polished shoes scuffling around and heard these guys whispering to each other in hushed tones, and we immediately ran down the hall and got the marshal, who was in charge of security at federal trials. The marshal burst through the closet door to find two guys with their briefcases open and their alligator clips on the terminals. They looked up and the marshal said, "You are under arrest," and I just about pissed my pants with pleasure—two FBI agents, and we caught them red-handed.

The cops came in, grabbed those wires, and ripped them off the terminals. The FBI agents slammed their briefcases shut, pulled out their credentials, and said, "You can't say anything to us. We're federal agents." The marshal, who was a truly good man, said to them, "Well, I'm a federal marshal. Come on out now. We're going straight to see the judge." So he brought them before Judge Arnow, and he told the judge what he had seen and what they had said. "The evidence is in that briefcase," he concluded. And Judge Arnow replied, "I don't need to see inside that briefcase. That briefcase is sealed. That's private property of the Federal Bureau of Investigation. We can't open it in this courtroom." The marshal looked at the judge in total disbelief. "You all are just trying to make a mountain out of a molehill," Judge Arnow added. The courtroom was full of members of the press from all over the country, and they all moaned out loud at his statement.

We left that night, and I drafted a statement right away for a press conference the next day. The story was already circulating in the press, because reporters had been present when that closet door swung open, and we knew this was going to be beautiful. It was going to be egg on the face of the FBI and the court. So I wrote a statement that kicked the shit out of that gag rule. This was the moment it had to be done, and we worked on it all night. Either I was going to stand up the next morning and say, "Boys, I ain't got the balls to do this," or I was going to stand up and dare them to arrest me. In the end, I chose the latter, and when I finished giving my statement, a journalist named Gloria Emerson, a correspondent for *The New York Times* both in Vietnam and at the trial who later wrote a book in 1976 about Vietnam called *Winners and Losers* that won the National Book Award—a legendary woman—came up to me and said, "I want a copy of that. That's one of the best things I've ever heard." This floored me. We, of course, had copies of the statement ready for the press, and it ran on the national news. I didn't see it, because I was in hiding, but people told me I was on CBS and that Walter Cronkite talked about us that night. People in Kansas saw it, too, and I had to deal with that later when I went back.

That night, the bench warrants were issued for my arrest. So I had to stay out of sight, while Bart Savage stepped up and took my place as spokesperson for the VVAW. I wanted to stay out of jail for as long as I could, long enough to go home and prepare for going to jail. We learned from the marshals that they weren't looking for me, at least not seriously, at the time. They said, "If he wants to go home, he should go ahead and do it." The group of attorneys who were representing us from the National Lawyers Guild went to the Fifth Circuit Court of Appeals in New Orleans to try to get the gag rule struck down, but the court wouldn't hear their arguments about freedom of speech. Judge Arnow's warrant stood, and it had a twelve-month statute of limitations, so for eleven and a half months I worked at a bookstore back home, wondering every day if marshals were going to show up to take me away. I made arrangements for my dogs to be taken care of, in the event that they came for me, and I warned my parents, "I may be going to prison." I remember my dad saying, "You asked for this." And I said, "No, I didn't ask for this, Dad. They put me in a ludicrous position, and I had to do it."

Eleven and a half months later, my lawyers called me and said, "The feds have been to the office. They are issuing warrants again and want to know if you want them to come up there or if you could just come down here to Florida." I thought to myself, *Jeez. I don't want to be arrested up here in front of people I know. Plus, if I turn myself in down there, I can go with Billy Richardson, my trusted friend.* So I called Billy, and he said, "I'll drive you down there." We had a lot of fun on the trip down to Gainesville, but the whole time I was thinking, *God, I hope all those stories about prison aren't true.* I was scared, because I wasn't a big guy, probably around 130 pounds at the time, and I knew I didn't stand a chance against bigger guys inside prison. I had been talking to people who had served time, trying to get a sense of what it would be like, and the more I learned, the more horrible it sounded. So I summoned all of my moral courage and braced myself for whatever was to come.

To my great relief, it all boiled down to optics in the end. If they put me away for speaking out, the government was going to be seen as trying to step on a disabled veteran from Kansas who refused to surrender his constitutional obligations and rights. When the pickup order was issued, the Department of Justice stepped in and got involved, setting it aside. According to my lawyers, they didn't want to embarrass a federal judge, so instead they decided the issue was moot, because the trial had ended in acquittal. So they abandoned the idea of bringing me in. This merciful use of "prosecutorial discretion" came as welcome news to me and to my parents, who had been worried sick about the prospect of visiting me in federal prison. The judge might have tried to gag me, but I was still free to speak against the war on behalf of my fellow veterans.

CHAPTER 15

—

Finding the Others

ONE OF THE HARDEST DECISIONS I had to make, about three years into my work with the VVAW, in the fall of 1973, was to leave the organization. After a period of nonstop adrenaline and conflict with the federal government, not to mention all of that national attention, I burned out and found myself at odds with leadership that didn't always share my values or sense of mission and were going politically in a direction with which I was no longer comfortable. When I made my break, I left behind the only organization that I'd ever been willing to join, other than the Marine Corps, and it left me a bit unmoored. I didn't know what my role was going to be or if I would even have one, living in a small town in Kansas, out of the limelight. I figured I would probably fade into obscurity, and I made my peace with that idea. What I didn't realize was that newspapers kept files. So I would still get calls from reporters asking for interviews after I left the VVAW, whenever anything came up that was related to Vietnam or Vietnam veterans, which kept me in the public eye. Also, I continued to get calls about speaking engagements, which was liberating, because I could finally say exactly what I thought, without having to worry about representing the views of the national office or the membership.

At first, I gave a lot of talks about the history of the VVAW and the movement. People were particularly interested in that because it was a unique moment in history, the only time that American veterans had come home and organized to protest a war in which they had fought while the war was going on. The movement was still ongoing, and the VVAW was still in the news occasionally, though it was getting more and more marginalized by its radicalism. I often fielded questions on why I left and on my views of the VVAW's current positions and activities, and I tried my best to tread carefully with my answers, because I didn't want it to seem as if I were at war with the organization. Nor did I wish to find myself pigeonholed into the role of being the disillusioned Vietnam veteran. So I would say, "Look, I'll give you the history as I know it, but I'm not going to editorialize it." I told them there were still a lot of people in the organization whom I admired, and I wasn't going to do anything to piss them off. Meanwhile, I tried my best to stay out of the fray, while working at that bookstore, and began building my library of Vietnam literature.

One thing I discovered at that time was just how hard it was for veteran writers to get published. It seemed as if any book about the war had a twelve-month shelf life. It would be published in hardback, last for about a year, and then would be cut loose. There were a few exceptions, of course, but it became my mission to make sure good books about the war were available to Vietnam veterans so they could see how their war was being portrayed and perhaps through literature find a language and a path back to reintegrating with society. We built up a hell of a clientele at that little bookstore, one of only two private bookstores in the town of Lawrence, Kansas. People started flocking there for books on military history and literature about Vietnam, and I met a lot of vets that way. I developed some friendships in the store that I still value to this day. Working in the bookstore also connected me with scores of Vietnam veterans who were sympathetic to the VVAW but simply were not joiners, and in a very unofficial and unorganized way we began forming groups of fellow veterans who just wanted to help one another. One of the most important roles I have played since the war has been connecting vets to other vets. What these guys really wanted was to be around each other so they could talk and tell their stories without being judged. At the time I started doing it, I felt as if I were walking around with only one boot on, because I didn't have an organization behind me, but I soon discovered that I didn't need an organization. All I needed was motivation and access.

This discovery, and the independence that came with it, led to other opportunities, to speak in public venues and for different veterans' groups, like the American Legion, that were not open to my views in the past, and slowly—so goddamn slowly— these organizations started opening up to me and began to address the issues faced by Vietnam veterans, things that at the time we thought were unique to us. The common perception of us was that we were broken and maladjusted, and many veterans from previous conflicts simply thought we weren't good Soldiers or warriors. Veterans' groups like the American Legion didn't believe in Post-Vietnam Syndrome, or PVS, at first. These vets looked down upon us, but many civilians thought even less of us, mostly because of how we were portrayed in the media. If a Vietnam veteran was convicted of a felony, then he made the front page of the newspaper, but if he did something good, he'd be lucky to be mentioned at all. In films and on television, we were almost uniformly portrayed as drug addicted and mentally unstable. And this made our relationship with the civilian world even more adversarial than it needed to be.

But I was in a unique position to address these perceptions head-on in a manner that would make people stop and think, *Now, wait a minute. That makes sense.* In speaking with diverse audiences, I found my role in helping the public understand who Vietnam veterans were, what we had done, the obstacles we'd faced, and what we were doing now. There was never a lack of civilian interest, because most civilians knew a Vietnam veteran in one way or another. He was a cousin or uncle or brother or relative, someone they went to school with that they were having trouble understanding. Sometimes, I'd meet guys at my talks who were closeted Vietnam vets, guys who had come home and burned their uniforms or buried them out of shame, and when I met them, I'd refuse to let them stay isolated, refuse to allow them to be forgotten. Whenever they revealed themselves to me at events, I saw my role as putting them in touch with other vets and helping them come into the light.

Sometimes, if I met someone who had been hiding the fact that he was a veteran, I'd try to connect him with his old unit, in order to get him to open up. "Hey," I'd say, "I know a couple of guys that were in the 101st, and maybe we ought to get together and shoot the shit about this stuff, you know?" It was shocking to be out in communities and to see how fragmented and alone we all were, because the war had become so unpopular. When people didn't want to talk with you and didn't want to know you, you could become awfully lonely so fast that you'd decide it was better not to say anything about your service. But I wasn't having any of that. I tried my best to be there for these guys, especially when they sought me out. The conversation would always start with "I don't give a shit about any of that. It's dead to me. I left all that behind and don't want to talk about it." But I never pushed or pried. They were there, and they were clearly eager just to have somebody to talk with who might understand. It was the most significant experience of our lives, and everyone in our society was telling us to bury it. It was nuts, and there was nothing healthy about it. I've always been an in-your-face vet, ever since that encounter in college when those other vets took me aside and told me, "Don't dress like a vet. Don't talk like a vet. Don't act like a vet." That was when I started dressing and acting like a vet, because I wasn't going to be made to feel ashamed of who I was. So I walked around with a pretty big chip on my shoulder, which turned out to be good for me and for my buddies.

Over the years, I've lost a good many friends who were consumed by guilt and shame and took their own lives. Each one of them was in his element talking to other veterans about the war. However, the war wasn't the only reason they committed suicide. It might have played a role, but one of the other contributing factors was the public reaction to the war, and the wholesale criminalization of Vietnam veterans. The way they were treated after they returned, not just by the antiwar movement, but by average Americans, came as the ultimate betrayal, and it caused my friends to feel isolated and alone and resulted in many of them seeing no other way to end their pain than to take their own lives. I tried to reach all of them, but there were many I couldn't reach, and there were plenty I walked away from feeling that I had utterly failed them. Then there were other times, years later, when I'd bump into a veteran who would say, "You know, you really helped me turn a corner," and it would make me feel as though all of my efforts had been worth it if I'd saved just one life. You never know when something you say or do might have that kind of impact on a person; this is what gave me hope in the face of my friends' suicides and deaths. A war might politically come to an end, but I've heard it said that a war isn't over until the last veteran dies, and so I made it my mission to serve my fellow veterans, to help them along the journey to healing that I had been on, until the day that I meet my Maker. It was an extraordinary experience for me. Selfishly, it kept me in touch with Vietnam veterans, and I was never more comfortable than when I was with other Vietnam vets.

One of the biggest challenges of that time came from within the veteran community. The Veterans of Foreign Wars, or VFW, and the American Legion spent so much time insulting the shit out of us, calling us crybaby vets when we talked about what is now called PTSD and other mysterious illnesses. They accused us of being after a quick buck from the VA and said that we had invented the whole Agent Orange myth to get attention, and then they wondered why we didn't rush to join them when we came home. At the time, people were just beginning to talk about post-traumatic stress disorder, though we didn't have a clinical name for it until much later. Originally, it was called Post-Vietnam Syndrome, and in 1972 the VVAW was the first veterans' organization to make PVS/PTSD and Agent Orange exposure a national priority. Around that same time, the VFW, the American Legion, AMVETS, and other organizations started seeing their membership dwindling and dying off because they had spent so much time denigrating and alienating Vietnam veterans, and they began to realize that their organizations didn't have much of a future. So they finally stepped in and got involved with Agent Orange and with PTSD, and as they picked up more of the slack on these issues, I began to pull back and focus on other things. I didn't turn down speaking engagements, but I wasn't being asked to speak as often, because people could now go to their local chapter and hear experts who were schooled on the issues talk about them with authority.

When I left the VVAW, I thought that was it, and I wouldn't be asked to speak anymore. But kids who heard me speak in their high schools were calling me to speak at their colleges and to other community groups, so leaving the VVAW actually gave me the opportunity to redirect my attention to the issues that I determined were most important. Number one among them was the prisoner of war issue, which became my primary focus in 1975, because the war wouldn't be over until everyone was home. The general public believed, wrongly, that everyone had come home from the war, but Operation Homecoming had clearly been a smoke-and-mirrors act, and when I began learning the factual history of the men who had been left behind, I was stunned at the evidence. When I read all of the declassified government documents about abandoned prisoners of war and began to register all of the lies that had been layered onto the issue, I turned all of my attention to exposing the POW issue for what it was to Americans, a complete and abject betrayal of our brothers and of everything we stood for as a country. This put me in touch with the families of POWs, whose courage was astonishing. They were willing to get their heads knocked, to be arrested and have criminal records, just to get the word out, because the news media wasn't interested in printing POW stories, which didn't fit into the tidy narrative that the war was over.

I joined these families and fellow activists in the movement to tell the American people that the war was anything but over. We resolved to build a national movement, not on an organizational level, but out of individual family members and veterans. What we accomplished was extremely powerful, and I wish it were still as powerful as it once was, but after that first decade it lost a lot of steam. We were able to organize tens of thousands of people to go to Washington and raise hell about the POW issue in the 1980s, and it's the one issue I will not back down from a single inch. I was not abandoned. I am alive because my buddies didn't abandon me. How could I allow the government to do what an eighteen-year-old Marine refused to allow to happen to me? How could I abandon others, when I wasn't abandoned myself? I spoke all over the country. Family members endorsed me, and that opened a lot of doors, and— even though many people rejected the POW issue and did not agree with my position—I never backed down.

Eventually, I developed a reputation as being the go-to guy for handling adversarial groups. People heard about my knowledge on the issue and my passion, and also my ability to reason with people who did not share my views, and they invited me to speak. Serving veterans, the ones who survived and the ones who were left behind, has been the most fulfilling work of my life. It has helped me shoulder the weight of the guilt that I felt for surviving the war to know that I was making a difference in veterans' lives and the lives of their families. By serving other veterans, listening to their stories, telling mine, and helping them and their loved ones to heal, I began the lifelong journey of healing myself.

A few years later, when I finally made plans to visit the Vietnam Veterans Memorial in Washington, D.C., I didn't know how I was going to feel. I had been apprehensive about seeing it from the beginning. The whole thing had been shrouded in controversy, like everything else surrounding the Vietnam War. But I decided I had to go judge for myself. I bought a ticket and steeled myself for the experience, summoning my courage and taking command of my thoughts like a Marine.

When I got to D.C. and approached the Reflecting Pool, I was immediately struck by the sheer number of names on those long, slanting granite walls rising up out of the earth. From a distance, there were so many names that they looked like a light gray abstract painting. As I moved closer and the names came into focus, they became an unfathomable reality. My throat swelled up, and I thought, *Oh, shit. I can't do this right now.* So I walked over to the statue called *The Three Soldiers* over on the side and tried to collect myself there. I hadn't even set foot in the memorial. I'd only seen it from a distance, and I felt as if I were going to faint.

A few minutes later, I pulled myself together and descended into the memorial to face what awaited me there. The first name I looked up was Doc Shade, and then I located Billy Petrossi. As soon as I found them, my legs went right out from under me, and I collapsed to the ground, sobbing. Of course, I knew they were dead, but something about seeing their names on the wall touched me to my core and helped me release feelings of sorrow and grief that I wasn't even aware were stored up in my body. I knelt there, crying, unable to catch my breath, completely overwhelmed by the experience. And in that moment, as hard as it was to bear, I was so grateful to God that the memorial was there. *This is going to save lives,* I thought. *Guys are going to come here and touch their friends' names, and it will help them stay alive.* We were losing so many Vietnam veterans in those days. We still are. Standing before the wall, for once I was speechless.

I couldn't find the words. But that was all right, because the memorial spoke for me. By holding the names of our dead or missing brothers and sisters within its majestic black granite, the wall helped us carry their memories forward, ensuring they would never be forgotten.

Coming Full Circle

A HUGE PIECE OF MY HEALING over the past twenty years has centered on helping not only Vietnam veterans and their families but also veterans of the most recent conflicts in Iraq and Afghanistan. One of the things I have discovered with age is that the half-life of trauma is decades, and some wounds get worse with time, not better. This is why the full brunt of the Vietnam War is only being felt now, more than fifty years later, as many of the veterans and civilians who experienced it find themselves confronting painful memories—in flashbacks and nightmares—that only seem to intensify with time. I went through hell when I first came home from war, so after the terrorist attacks on 9/11 and the subsequent invasions of Afghanistan and Iraq, I vowed that I would do everything in my power to help combat veterans returning from the recent wars so they wouldn't feel as abandoned and alone as I had when I came home.

A few years into the wars in Iraq and Afghanistan, while we

were losing thousands of brave young American kids overseas and our troops started coming home with visible and invisible wounds, I began getting asked to speak on the subject of PTSD and combat-related trauma again. My work with the current generation of vets really didn't take off until 2007, when I was asked to speak at a Fourth of July celebration in a little town called Pratt, Kansas. They wanted me to talk about my experience both as a combat veteran and as someone who struggles with post-traumatic stress. After I spoke, these two Soldiers, Major Jeff Hall and Captain Josh Mantz, stood up and talked about their experiences, and we immediately hit it off. They were both stationed at Fort Riley in Manhattan, Kansas, home of the First Infantry Division, or the "Big Red One." Before I knew it, they got me a speaking gig on post, and the deputy commander, Brigadier General David Petersen, invited me to come talk to his command and address the units that were just arriving home from Iraq, on their family day. This was a little uncomfortable for me at first, because I knew what these Soldiers were thinking: *Who the hell is this guy? And why do I have to listen to him? I'm with my family here. I just got home.* Fortunately, they did listen to what I had to say, and they were very kind and open with me. So that led to a number of other speaking engagements on post, and it also led to Josh's and my setting up a counseling program off post through a program for wounded warriors at Fort Riley.

At that time in the U.S. Armed Forces, it was seen as a career-ending gesture for a Soldier to raise his hand and say, "I'm struggling with an invisible wound." Most of these guys were suffering in silence until we set up the program, and even then, when they started bringing in Soldiers by the van loads to us, they were still apprehensive about receiving mental health treatment, even off base with civilian providers. These were all career Soldiers, and in order to accept our help, they had to trust us with their careers. We decided to start meeting at a barbecue restaurant that my wife, Shannon, and I liked a lot. We knew the owners and contacted them to see if they could provide us with a private room upstairs. When I explained to them what we were trying to do, they said, "Well, hey, just take the entire upstairs. It's yours. Go up there and have your meetings." We'd convene up there pretty regularly over these big, sprawling barbecue dinners. I'd bring up a large group of Vietnam veterans for each session, and we established right from the get-go that there were no Vietnam vets and no Iraq vets and no Afghanistan vets in the room. There were just combat veterans, and some of us were older than the others. My reason for bringing up fellow Vietnam veterans was to give the younger guys examples of coping strategies and tactics that we had used when nobody else was there to help us, and to show them that many of us had still managed to become successful, in spite of how we were treated by our fellow Americans and by the VA. After those first few sessions, which were some of the most gratifying intergenerational exchanges I'd ever experienced, Josh Mantz assured us that our program was the most effective one he had participated in at Fort Riley.

Of course, it helped all of us. Every Vietnam veteran involved was convinced that the sessions with the Iraq and Afghanistan veterans were helping us as much as they were helping them. We had to be able to stand behind what we said, because these younger guys could smell bullshit from a mile away. These were career NCOs, and if they thought we were bullshitting them, they would have blown us off. But they knew we were on the level, and we asked as many questions as we answered. Sometimes, they'd even offer ideas that they thought might help us, and we'd listen to them with open minds. We made it a give-and-take. There were some pretty substantial differences between our experiences. A few of the Vietnam vets had done more than one tour, but we hadn't racked up anywhere near the number of tours or the kinds of tours some of these kids had. They didn't have a draft, and so an all-volunteer force of active-duty military that represents less than 1 percent of the American population has now borne the brunt of these wars for an unconscionably long time. But combat is combat is combat is combat. You don't have to assault an NVA position to be trau-matized by it. All you have to do is see buddies be killed or be wounded yourself to be traumatized in any number of ways. Or come home, after seeing combat, to a cheating spouse or a bro-ken family. There are countless paths to loneliness, anger, and isolation, and we wanted these kids to know that they were not alone. The country was more than willing to express its grati-tude to these guys, to thank them for their service, in ways that we were never thanked, but the country had no idea what they were asking of these kids. So all of the expressions of gratitude and support wore a little thin for them. We tried to help them gain some perspective by describing how we were treated when we came home.

During some of these sessions, I opened up about the chal-lenges I faced after coming back from Vietnam, sharing how I spent most of my twenties and thirties struggling with demons, burning through relationships, driving my car and my motor-cycle really fast, and getting into horrible wrecks, chasing after the adrenaline rush that I had first felt in combat. Other than riding my motorcycle, I wasn't able to find anything that made life taste good enough until I started jumping out of planes. I've

Me, Jay, and Butch on a motorcycle trip in the late 1980s or early 1990s.

never found anything that was as pure and as honest as skydiving. I dedicated over twenty years of my life to the sport and it got me through some pretty tough times. You can't bullshit in free fall, in the same way that you can't bullshit in combat.

Some of the Soldiers from Fort Riley would, in turn, open up to me about their own struggles with depression, and I would tell them about how I had wrestled with suicidal thoughts for close to two decades after my return. I gave up on having a future in the bush, I would tell them, and it wasn't until I was thirty-six and my first son, Daniel, was born that things turned around. When I witnessed his first moments in this world, I had my last thought of ending my life, because all of a sudden I could conceive of the future again. It wasn't my future. It was my son's, and I had to stay alive to be there for him. We did a lot of talking in those sessions about the things that helped ground us in the present moment and helped us see the future.

Me skydiving.

When Soldiers spoke about their marital problems, I'd talk plainly with them about my first marriage, which ended in divorce, and encourage them not to give up hope, sharing with them how it took years for me to find the person who had the sensitivity, courage, and emotional fortitude to love me for who I am. My second wife, Shannon, I'd tell them, has been one of the most significant parts of my journey back to life, health, and wholeness. When we started seeing each other, I was a complete mess and was about as paranoid as I could be about getting remarried, but she had a deep understanding of what it meant to be in a relationship with a combat veteran, and her support for me has been unconditional and unwavering. She had grown up in a military family. Her father had done two tours in Vietnam, and so she understood me on a very deep level.

Ever since Shannon and I got married, I'd tell the guys, it just keeps getting better. When we started seeing each other,

Shannon had to nurse me back to health, because at that time my post-traumatic stress was beating the shit out of me. But she waded right into those waters with me. She rolled up her sleeves and got in, and slowly I overcame my fear of being vulnerable and trusted that our marriage would last. She is still as supportive now as she was then, and we've been married now for more than twenty years. In addition to being a nurse, Shannon is a wonderful writer, and we have spent the better part of the past two decades writing poetry together. We've written through some very tough times, and we've read each other's poems, providing feedback and cheering each other on. What she has written has given me strength, and I hope that what I've written has given her strength, too. Through writing and facing our darkest memories and fears, we've made a life together, one that I didn't think possible for much of my adulthood.

From time to time, when Soldiers opened up about their fears of seeking help and talking to mental health professionals, I'd tell them about how hard it had been for me to accept assistance from the people and the system that I felt had betrayed me and my buddies, but also how it had been worth it in the end. Vietnam veterans learned early that the VA was not our friend. We had to fight it on everything we got, and I didn't trust it. A number of VA hospitals in the late 1960s and early 1970s were caught treating veterans like shit and leaving them to die in their care, just like today. And so when I finally went for help, I was so shaken up about it that I had to have a buddy walk me into the Topeka, Kansas, VA and stay with me throughout the day. Going to the VA that day and making myself vulnerable turned out to be one of the best decisions of my life, because I met and ended up working with a wonderful psychiatrist named Dr. Carol Padilla, a fine doctor whom I came to trust.

Dr. Padilla has helped me a lot over the years. One of the things she helped me to see was that it was up to me to decide whether my experience in Vietnam was one of the most negative experiences in my life or a positive one.

The biggest thing I had to deal with after my time in the Marine Corps, I often told Soldiers, was survivor's guilt, though I didn't learn the name for it until years later. Every day I struggled with the question of why I was still alive and my buddies weren't. I was ashamed of surviving. And, in the early days, I was dealing with some pretty serious PTSD, although it would be another twenty-five years before doctors started calling it that. One day, Dr. Padilla had me sit down and write a list of all the things that made the war negative, about three or four pages long. Then she had me write down what was positive. I wrote only two words, "my buddies," and I didn't need to write anything else. In that moment, I saw something clearly, perhaps for the first time. *How could I have served with guys like that and then decide it was a negative experience?* It was an absolute honor to know them, and I shudder to think who I would be if I hadn't met them. This sudden new perspective came as a great relief, helped me to see my time in Vietnam as one of the most positive experiences of my life, and empowered me to celebrate all of the growth that came from all the loss. Even now, it's amazing to think that those brief but seemingly eternal eleven and a half months defined the rest of my life and made me the person I am today. Now, whenever someone walks up and thanks me for my service, I simply reply without hesitating, "It was a privilege."

After spending as much time as I have with combat veterans of the recent wars, I've never felt it more necessary to speak out than I do right now. I feel a responsibility to tell the American people about what's going on, that we haven't won a war since

1945. Desert Storm sure wasn't a victory. We left Saddam Hussein in his palace and didn't lift a finger as he slaughtered his own people. And for two decades we've been fighting wars on the cheap, placing the load of these conflicts on the backs of the working class, while most Americans, without a draft, have remained untouched. These conflicts have come at no cost to the majority of our citizens. Because of this, we have a whole new generation of disillusioned warriors coming home, and we can't afford another generation of disillusioned warriors. So I feel that it is a moral obligation to speak out. I talk at high school assemblies, I speak in college classes, and I bend the ears of ordinary Americans everywhere to talk about what we need to do as citizens to make this country right, to make it worthy of these kids who have returned from Iraq and Afghanistan.

I will never forgive the government for what it has done. Never. Not when I think about Vietnam and the sixty thousand dead Americans, and the millions of innocent civilians, who died for what? So we could say we kept our commitments? Because we didn't. Not when I think about the wars in Iraq and Afghanistan and the thousands of troops who have died, as well as the more than thirty thousand who've been wounded and would have died in any previous conflict but will now live long, challenging lives with complex injuries of the mind, body, and spirit. Not when I think of all the POWs we left behind in Southeast Asia. And not when I think about the countless veterans and their families still struggling to get decent health care from the broken VA system and just compensation for their sacrifices. Not when I think about how we fought the Second Battle of Fallujah in 2004, only to see it overtaken by ISIS ten years later, and it felt like 1973 all over again. Given the state of our world and the state of our country, we must remain vigilant and never forget our past, because the stakes are simply too high. If we don't speak out and hold our government account-able, we'll find ourselves in yet another land war in some other far-flung region of the world sacrificing American blood and treasure again, and for what . . . or for whom?

In 2017, I was given the opportunity to return to Vietnam. The trip was made possible by people from all over the world who had seen me in the 2017 PBS documentary *The Vietnam War*, directed by Ken Burns and Lynn Novick, who then con-tributed to a GoFundMe campaign started by friends. There had been an outpouring of support from countless people I did not know but who were moved by my story, and I was deeply moved by their kindness and generosity. The group that went over included my wife, Shannon; my oldest son, Daniel; Bill Tuttle, a retired professor from the University of Kansas I have known since 1971; John Solbach, a fellow Vietnam veteran and former congressman from Kansas; and Lindsey Foat, a trusted friend who worked as a production assistant at Kansas City Public Television in the ramp-up to the *Vietnam War* series.

From the moment we landed, we hit the ground running, moving at a steady gallop, spending a day in Hanoi and a night in Ha Long Bay, flying down to the city of Hue, and then travel-ing to Dong Ha. We spent three days in Quang Tri Province, on the north-central coast, returned to Hue, then moved on to Saigon for a day before we had to fly back to the States. For most of the trip, I was just a tourist, but during our short time in Quang Tri Province, I was able to make two trips to Con Thien in search of my Vietnam.

Over those two days, I scoured the earth for some trace of my time in Vietnam. To my immense disappointment, I could find nothing. It was as if the place in which I had fought and starved and bled and lost friends had never existed. I was not able to gain access to Con Thien, now protected by a government fence, and when I got out to what I thought was the place my company had been ambushed and I had been shot, I found it unrecognizable. What had been dense, overgrown jungle in November 1967 was now cultivated and flat and bore no resemblance to what I remembered. The landscape had completely changed, and as much as I yearned to feel a connection, I could not relate to it in any way.

We traveled to the Ba Long valley, but I wasn't able to find the position where we had actually been fighting, because we didn't have time. And when we arrived in Khe Sanh, I could not believe my eyes. When I had been there, Khe Sanh had been a small outpost in an unpopulated valley, with a little village. Now it was a full-fledged city. And the largely deserted road we used to call Ambush Alley or Colonial Route 9 is now a brand-new highway with houses and habitation all along it. There used to be an enormous airstrip in Khe Sanh, and when our group visited the little museum there, with exhibits and plaques commemorating the "glorious victory over the Marines," a museum docent walked up to me and asked if I wanted to see it. I said, "Hell yeah!" and he opened this door, and we walked outside, and he just stopped. I looked around, completely disoriented, and said, "Where's the airstrip?" He pointed down a small dirt path and said, "It's right here."

Before I left on the trip, a friend of mine who had been a Donut Dolly, a Red Cross volunteer in Vietnam, whose brother had been a Marine lieutenant who was killed in action right after she returned from the war, offered me a piece of advice. "If you're going over there to mourn your Vietnam," she warned me, "be ready not to find it." At the time, I had no idea what she meant, but standing at the end of that dirt path in Khe Sanh, I understood. Intellectually, I knew where I was, but emotionally I was lost, and it made me incredibly angry.

When our guide had first driven us up to Con Thien, stopped the van, opened the door, and said, "Well, there's Con Thien," I looked at him and said, "Bullshit!" I was pissed. I started to freak out. I thought they were trying to play a trick on me, and I said, "No, no, no. This isn't Con Thien! I lived here twice." But our guide insisted, "Yes, yes, it is Con Thien. I swear!" So I got out of the van and started looking around, and slowly it began to dawn on me: *Holy shit. This is Con Thien.*

Con Thien was unique because it was a three-topped hill. It was only about five hundred feet high, but it was the only high ground in the area near the DMZ, less than two miles from North Vietnam, which was why so many people had fought and died there on both sides. When we first pulled up in the van, all I could see was a forest of tall trees, but I soon realized that I was looking at a group of short trees on a tall hill. As hard as I squinted my eyes, I could not see the Con Thien where I had once lived through the branches and the leaves. I wasn't permitted to go there, either. The best I could do was stand on the perimeter and gaze in the direction of where it once had been.

I turned to the group and told them that if we had been standing in that spot in 1967, we would be dead. The Marine Corps had strewn tens of thousands of mines around Con Thien, and it would not have been possible to walk more than a few feet without setting one of them off. I began telling them the story, which I had never before shared with Shannon or Daniel, of the three-man listening post that got lost while going outside the wire right in front of my hole. It was moonless and pitch-black in the middle of monsoon season, and right when they got twenty meters deep into the field, a kid in the middle stepped on a Bouncing Betty. I told them how mines sound different from other explosives, and whenever someone steps on a mine, there's always a moment of silence after the explosion before the screaming starts. Just as I finished telling them this, a mine went up about a hundred meters to the south of where we were standing. My heart clenched, and everyone looked at me in horror as they realized what the sound meant. There were laborers working around the rubber trees that surrounded Con Thien, and at least one of them, who had tripped an old mine, was either dead or severely injured. I was waiting through the silence for the screams. Shannon immediately went into nurse mode, and we started moving in the direction of the sound and I kept thinking, *I don't want to see this. I don't want to have to see this again.* But I couldn't stop myself from going. We had to try. But before we could get past the perimeter, we were told they had found a mine and blown it up. To our great relief, no one had stepped on it. It had been purposefully detonated. Still, the timing had been uncanny. The explosion had been an exclamation mark at the end of my story.

As much as I wished to revisit my Vietnam, I wasn't able to find it. Though my heart ached to visit with those North Vietnamese veterans, I wasn't able to speak with them. Lynn Novick had tried to arrange for me to meet with a group of veterans over there, who apparently were as eager as I was to connect, but the Vietnamese government prohibited them from speaking with me, likely because of the state media's disapproval of the *Vietnam War* series. In returning to Vietnam, I had hoped to do emotionally what I had done intellectually through my writing and speaking about the war. In my collection *Notes to the Man Who Shot Me,* I had written a poem of the same title in

which I tried to put aside the hatred that consumed me during
and after the war:

> I have often
> thought of
> you
> all these years
> and
> hated you
> for using me
> as bait
> but the truth is . . .
> had our roles
> been reversed
> I would have done the same
> I wish now
> that I could
> talk to you
> I wonder how I looked
> to you
> I wonder, were you as terrified
> as I was?
> I wonder, did you hate me
> as much as I hated you?
> I wonder how long you'd been
> fighting your war
> I wonder if you had any children
> And, I wonder had you survived
> and we met today
> would you speak to me?
> I sometimes imagine

us meeting again
and talking about that ambush
while our children play together
You were a good soldier
I've come to realize
that you and I
had more in common
than we did
with the men who sent us
to kill each other
If I could,
I would give you the gift
I have longed for
all these years,
The gift of peace

Me at Con Thien, 2019. Photo credit: Daniel Musgrave.

For years, I had confused hatred with loyalty to the memories of my fallen buddies. And so when I wrote that poem, I had come to the conclusion, in my head, that hatred had no place in my life. But in my gut, I couldn't let go of the hatred, and your gut gets a vote.

It wasn't until I watched *The Vietnam War* and saw those North Vietnamese veterans who had once fought against me in battle, and listened to their stories, that I realized they were old men, just like me, and I could relate to them in a new way. The nineteen-year-old boys who haunted my dreams were my age now. I wanted to sit down with them and look them in the eyes. I wanted to embrace them and to tell them I was glad they were alive. I wanted to declare peace, for them and for me, and know in my heart that I no longer had to carry the weight I had been carrying for more than fifty years. I did not need to carry it, and my buddies would never have wanted me to carry it. But in my heart, I am standing on the perimeter of Con Thien, unable to see through the trees.

Acknowledgments

No one makes it through their lives without the assistance of many others.

My brother, Ken (also known as Butch), and I were born to hardworking and loving parents who raised us to be grateful for our good fortune, for our family, and for our community and to be good citizens for our country.

I wouldn't have made it through adolescence without friends like my brother and Larry Jones, Jay Van Velzen, Steve Wright, Dennis Stopplemore, Henry Heflin, my cousin Richard Musgrave, and countless others.

During my time in the Marine Corps, Jim Murray, Dan Cooney, Pat Van Buren, Jim Rye, Leonard Blair, George Shade, Jack Hartzel, Sam Smith, and Skip Sconzo, and, especially, Lieutenant Magee kept me going. Sometimes, literally.

Those first difficult years at home and in college I only survived due to the love and patience of people like Bill Richardson, Alan Miller, Geoff Nichols, and Don Brower.

The difficult years in the VVAW would have been unbearable without the support of brothers like Scott Camil, Johnie Upton, Jon Birdsal, and Ron Sable.

Over many years working on veterans' issues and the Live POW Movement, I feel I owe the most to the Britt Small and Festival family, whose music, dedication to the veterans' movement, and professional sacrifices were nothing short of heroic. It was an honor working with them all.

To lifelong friends in the Midwest skydiving community, I wish heartfelt "Blue Skies" to you all: Rance Sackrider, Phil McAbee, Richard McCarthy, Tim Ericson, Rusty Young, Eric Peck, and many others.

To Brian Daldorph, mentor and editor, whose belief in my poetry led me here, I owe a debt of artistic gratitude. Looking forward to many more years of friendship and collaboration.

A special mention needs to be made of Rose Marino and David Hann, as well as David Clark and all the generous people who made our dream of returning to Vietnam a reality. It could never have happened without you.

There are so many others that deserve mention for their friendship, support, and encouragement over the years: Camille Williamson, Mike Clodfelter, Kathy and Jim Brothers, Rob Bergmann, Roger LaRue, Teresa Gibson, Carol Hall, Mona and Sean, Paul Dorrell, Kayler Bole, Gil Sanborn, Jim Fontaine, Melinda Hipple, Larry Butell, Lindsey Foat, John Solbach, Mike and Ruth McGraw, Kirk Allison, Tom "Doc" Berger, Jo Gault, Harvey and Diane Nicholson, and Richard Sosinski. If you played a significant role in my life and do not find your name here, our stories might have been edited out, or I've worried that, for various reasons, you might not want to be mentioned and I tried to respect your privacy.

To Chris, thank you for our beautiful sons. To my wife, Shannon, thank you for our beautiful daughters, as well as our sustaining marriage and happy home. Every chapter in this book has benefited from your input.

To my children, Lilian, Daniel, Rye, and Maddy, and our granddaughter, Elsie Rose, I know it wasn't easy growing up with a combat veteran father and grandfather. I hope this will help explain why Dad *still* needs that night-light.

To my in-laws, Pat and A. D. Woods, thank you for dedicating twenty years of your lives to the service of our country and for making me feel a part of a wonderful family.

This book is the result of the belief held by Ken Burns and Lynn Novick that people should know more of my story. I owe them more than I can possibly express here. I'd also like to thank Salimah El-Amin and Lucas Frank of Florentine Films for their help with the photographs in this book, along with everyone at Florentine Films who made the *Vietnam War* series possible, with special thanks to the producer Sarah Botstein and the writer Geoffrey C. Ward.

When I was first approached by Ken about the project, I told him that I could not write a book like this. I'm a poet, but something like this was beyond my writing abilities. He asked if I would feel comfortable telling my story to a writer. We both felt that might work, and there was one writer we knew and were both comfortable with, Bryan Doerries. I had worked with Bryan a few times on his extraordinary project, Theater of War, and I had read his book on the project. I already knew and trusted Bryan as a friend, and I knew that if he had the desire and the time to collaborate, we could make it work. The process of getting this story to Bryan, who lives in New York City, from my home in a small town in Kansas was two-fold. Bryan interviewed me over the phone, and we spent many hours together that way, going back and forth, with him asking questions of me that he needed answered. I also taped hours of stories on my own and forwarded them to him.

To facilitate this process, Ken and Lynn arranged for my introduction to Jay Mandel at WME (many thanks for his wonderful representation in the "foreign" world of publishing). Thanks also to the agent Zoë Pagnamenta for her steady-handed support and to Sally Arteseros for her help with the manuscript. My sincere gratitude also goes to Andrew Miller and Maris Dyer at Knopf for their guidance, dedication, and professionalism.

Special mention needs to be made here of two young veterans, Jeff

Hall and Josh Matz, who arranged for me to work with veterans of the First Infantry Division at Fort Riley, Kansas, and who asked me to participate in Bryan Doerries's Theater of War project. After meeting me and hearing my story, Bryan introduced me to Ken Burns and Lynn Novick, with the hope that they might interview me for their film. Without Jeff and Josh, none of this would have happened.

I'd like to thank Marjolaine Goldsmith for her meticulous transcription. This extraordinary young woman listened and transcribed hours and hours of my memories. She learned about Marine Corps boot camp in the sixties, from thumping turds to doing the chicken. She also learned about the horrors of the bush, from enduring the leeches to combat with the NVA. She had to listen to some of it through my tears. I've worried that she hears my voice in her sleep and that she also shares my nightmares.

And, finally, to Bryan Doerries, trusted friend and dedicated writer, who somehow took my memories and created this book: I am amazed. I am so grateful. I'm literally the luckiest man I've ever known. Thanks, buddy.

A NOTE ABOUT THE AUTHOR

John Musgrave served in Vietnam for eleven months and seventeen days in both the First and the Third Marine Divisions before being permanently disabled by his third wound. He was medically retired as a corporal in 1969. He is the recipient of two Purple Hearts and two Vietnamese Crosses of Gallantry. In addition to speaking publicly about his war experiences, and working with younger veterans to help them reintegrate and heal, Musgrave is the author of the collection *Notes to the Man Who Shot Me: Vietnam War Poems*.

A NOTE ON THE TYPE

This book was set in Hoefler Text, a family of fonts designed by Jonathan Hoefler, who was born in 1970. First designed in 1991, Hoefler Text was intended as an advancement on existing desktop computer typography, including as it does an exponentially larger number of glyphs than previous fonts. In form, Hoefler Text looks to the old-style fonts of the seventeenth century, but it is wholly of its time, employing a precision and sophistication only available in the late twentieth century.

Composed by North Market Street Graphics, Lancaster, Pennsylvania
Printed and Bound at Friesens, Altona, Canada
Designed by Maggie Hinders